W9-BVV-839

The Color of Teaching

One of the major concerns in education at present is how to recruit and attract more teachers of color to the profession. In an attempt to move beyond the superficial and simplistic responses as to why students of color are not entering teaching, *The Color of Teaching* presents in-depth interviews with over two hundred persons of color from four ethnic groups: African Americans, Native Americans, Asian Americans and Latinos in the United States.

These interviewees, many of them teachers or education professionals, express their attitude towards teaching and their understanding of why students of color may not be selecting teaching as a career.

One of the most significant and surprising findings is that, regardless of academic or socio-economic standing, students of color tend not to be encouraged to enter the teaching profession by their own families, communities, and peers. The book concludes with a discussion of programmatic changes and calls for the reconceptualization of the role of teachers. Such changes can only arise out of a fundamental change in attitude of communities of color towards teaching which must be led by teachers themselves.

The Color of Teaching will appeal to a wide audience of teachers in training and in practice, educational policy makers, and educational administrators.

June A. Gordon is Assistant Professor of Education at the University of California, Santa Cruz. She teaches courses in social and cultural diversity with an emphasis on urban education. Her research focuses on the various factors that hinder the access and success of marginalized students in the United States, England, and Japan.

Educational Change and Development Series
Andy Hargreaves
Ontario Institute for Studies in Education, Canada
Ivor F. Goodson
Warner Graduate School, University of Rochester, USA and
Centre for Applied Research in Education, University of East
Anglia, Norwich, UK

The Color of Teaching

June A. Gordon

BISHOP MUELLER LIBRARY
Briar Cliff University
SIOUX CITY, IA 51104

London and New York

First published 2000 by RoutledgeFalmer
11 New Fetter Lane, London EC4P 4EE

Simultaneously published in the USA and Canada
by RoutledgeFalmer
29 West 35th Street, New York, NY 10001

RoutledgeFalmer is an imprint of the Taylor & Francis Group

© 2000 June A. Gordon

Typeset in Times by Taylor & Francis Books Ltd
Printed and bound in Great Britain by
TJ International Ltd, Padstow, Cornwall

All rights reserved. No part of this book may be reprinted or
reproduced or utilized in any form or by any electronic,
mechanical, or other means, now known or hereafter
invented, including photocopying and recording, or in any
information storage or retrieval system, without permission in
writing from the publishers.

British Library Cataloguing in Publication Data
A catalogue record for this book is available from the British Library

Library of Congress Cataloging in Publication Data
Gordon, June A., 1950–
The color of teaching/June A. Gordon
Educational change and development series
Includes bibliographical references and index
1. Minority teachers–Recruiting–United States.
2. Minorities–Education–Social aspects–United States.
3. Teaching–Social aspects–United States. I. Title. II. Series.
LB2835.25.G67   2000
331.7'613711–dc21   99-055626

ISBN 0–750–70997–9 (hbk)
ISBN 0–750–70996–0 (pbk)

BK
₮24.91

Contents

Jones.6226. EDUC. 2491

Foreword

John U. Ogbu

This book addresses the important problem of increasing the participation of minorities in the teaching profession. Dr Gordon approaches the problem through a comparative study of community forces that potentially influence the decision of minorities to become teachers. Community forces are the ideas or images of teachers and the teaching profession held by members of a minority community or group.

Researchers have examined structural and institutional barriers that limit minority entry into the profession. Dr Gordon, however, believes that in order to fully understand why more minorities do not choose teaching as a career option, we have to study the community forces that influence their decisions. Minorities develop an image of the teaching profession from their own experiences in the educational system, especially with teachers, as well as from their perceptions of career options. The author argues that adults communicate to children images of teachers and the teaching profession as well as their hopes of future careers for them. Teachers also help shape children's images through the way they present themselves and their profession. Thus, both community forces and teachers influence children's decisions to become or not to become teachers. The comparative study covered four major minority groups: African American, Asian American, Latino American and Native American. Teachers from these groups were interviewed in Cincinnati in Ohio, Long Beach in California, and Seattle in Washington. Additional interviews with Asian American community members in the San Francisco Bay Area were conducted to offset the low number of available Asian American teachers.

Dr Gordon's research strongly suggests that community forces can potentially influence the choice of becoming teachers by minorities. The findings also demonstrate the importance of the comparative approach; although the groups share several factors in the community forces, there are also significant differences.

An important factor in developing a positive or negative image of the teaching profession is an individual's or group's historical experience with public schooling. Although these groups differ in specific encounters with the public schools, nonetheless those of African Americans, Latinos, and Native Americans have been, according to the author 'fraught with similar hostility, misunderstanding and distrust.' The Asian Americans interviewed, in contrast, did not see schooling as oppositional. This, however, does not mean that Asian Americans have not encountered conflicts with the schools; for example, earlier Asian immigrants experienced a great deal of conflict in educating their children in San Francisco.

Dr Gordon discusses community forces in terms of 'sociocultural factors.' These include perceptions of racism, cultural differences in the images of the teaching profession, and how minorities interpret the educational process. African American teachers believe that their people's experience of racism in K-12 schooling discourages them from considering teaching as a career since it would require them to return to the site of their struggle: the classroom. Native Americans, however, speak the most passionately about racism and how the mislabeling of their children has had a profound affect on school completion, undermining an interest in teaching. Latino teachers also point to high drop-out rates, based partially on the low expectations of counselors and teachers, in stalling the academic progress of their students and, hence, their ability to consider teaching as a career. Asians are primarily confounded by the complex demands placed on teachers in the US which are unrelated to academics.

The way minority groups interpret schooling in terms of their collective identity plays a major role in their decisions to become teachers. For some, schooling is a source of conflict threatening family and traditional values. It is an experience marked by what one Native American teacher calls 'cultural dissonance with the White man's ways.' This interpretation of schooling discourages minorities from going into teaching in two ways. One is that it discourages good academic performance which is crucial for admission into college preparation and quality performance in the teaching profession. The other is that families and communities with this perception discourage their members from going into teaching.

The connection between success in school and choice of teaching varies in form among the ethnic groups represented by the teachers interviewed. The most important school factor for African Americans, Latinos and Native Americans, but not for Asian Americans, is the inadequate academic preparation of minority students at pre-college level. Latino teachers believe that a major reason for the paucity of Latinos going into teaching is their poor academic achievement at precollege level and the low graduation rates. Native American teachers feel the same way. The specific reasons for the lack of good academic preparation include misplacement of children in ELS/LED language classes, inability to use their primary languages, being ostracized by peers who think that those who do well in school are not authentically Latinos, Native Americans, etc. Because of these experiences potential minority teachers either do not meet requirements for admission to teacher training programs or have difficulty passing teacher competency tests. Latino parents and community also expressed concern that the more education their children have or the longer they stay in school, the more they are alienated from their traditional values, customs, and community. For Native Americans, schooling may be interpreted as going to 'learn how to be a White man.' Among African Americans, the informants stated that students may not understand or value the career options that depend upon good academic performance. The author argues that interpretations like these can result in alienation from schooling and/or a sense of betrayal of one's family and group related to the choice of teaching as a profession. The Asian American community discourages its members from going into teaching in a different way. These immigrant minorities arrive in the United States with a positive pre-emigration image of teachers and the teaching profession which is in sharp contrast with the negative images they discover perpetuated in American society. Dr Gordon informs us that the low status of American teachers in combination with high standards for teachers within Asian cultures constitutes one of the major reasons for Asian American students not choosing teaching as a career option.

Teachers from the four minority groups go on to discuss at length the issues of image, respect, and status of the teaching profession and how these factors discouraged teaching as a career option in their respective communities. The author cautions that these factors are complex and interrelated. African Americans believe that the teaching profession in integrated American society does not have as high a status as it once had in their community prior to 1970. One reason is that mainstream America perceives teaching as a low-paying, low-status job. Another reason given by African Americans for loss of status and respect for teachers is the practice by many white teachers in inner-city schools to attempt to align themselves with their students by dressing informally and creating non-hierarchical relationships with their students. Like African Americans, Asian Americans are concerned with visible status: they generally prefer fields which pay more money and confer more prestige. Latino teachers do not consider low pay to be the main discouragement of Latinos from entering the teaching profession. This group, in fact, thinks that teaching pays well when compared to other jobs requiring comparable education. Likewise, economic reward does not appear to be a major impediment for Native Americans in considering teaching as a career.

The teachers have some ideas of their own about how to increase minority representation in the teaching profession. All emphasize the importance of a strong academic preparation of students in K-12 grades. As one teacher put it, 'Preparation is the key.' Some African American, Latino and Native American teachers would consider recruiting minorities to teach in schools where the students come mostly from their own groups. Asian American teachers do not share this view; race-matched teaching was not of significance. Three suggestions made to increase the numbers of minorities entering the teaching profession include: first, teachers and minority communities become more aware of the powerful influence they have in discouraging youth from entering the teaching profession and how this will play itself out in future generations; second, parents and teachers support academic engagement and achievement; and third, help students make the historical connections between the importance that education has made to their predecessors and how they can contribute to the success of future generations.

I share Dr Gordon's view that community forces can potentially influence the decisions of minority students to become teachers. We already know about various structural and institutional barriers. What we do not yet know about are the community forces. One important contribution of the present work is to draw our attention to their existence and potential influence. This study, therefore, opens a new area of inquiry for knowledge that can be used for policy and practices to increase the representation of minorities in the teaching profession. I hope that future researchers will include more non-teachers, such as minority students as well as non-teacher members of minority communities. The inclusion of wider representation from the minority community will increase our knowledge of the range of community forces.

Acknowledgements

I have been blessed with the support of some very special people who continue to find time and space in their busy lives to stay in touch, to read my work, and to be available when needed. I am especially grateful to John U. Ogbu, John I. Goodlad, Michael Knapp, Johnnella Butler and Barbara Gottesman.

While not one of Ogbu's students, I am indebted to him not only for his professional contributions to the field that have assisted me in framing my own inquiry but also for his continued support. Without his encouragement and prodding, this book might never have materialized.

But then if it had not been for Goodlad's invitation to be one of his last graduate students, I might never have pursued the academic course that led me to this work. Goodlad's genuine interest in my research (on the impediments that working-class students and students of color face in moving through the system) and his offer to assist both financially and academically in my doctoral study afforded me the opportunity to not only conduct the type of research I felt most suitable but also to work at the Center for Educational Renewal as his research assistant.

To Michael Knapp I offer my immense appreciation for his unstinting high standards of excellence and his belief that I could match up to them. Through the years, the lines between mentor, colleague, and friend have gradually blurred, only increasing my respect for someone who gives so willingly of himself.

To Johnnella Butler I attribute my more extensive reading in the area of American Ethnic Studies. As director of such a program at the University of Washington and a leading consultant on Transformative Curriculum, Johnnella stimulated my intellectual growth while simultaneously validating what I had already accomplished.

In addition to these academic mentors, the research for this book would never have been possible if not for the numerous teachers and community members who offered their time and stories to provide an important lens through which to understand the shortage of students of color in colleges of education and the role that community forces play in influencing young people's career decision making. Their trust in me and my students as well as their desire to have their voices heard are the driving forces that have propelled this book forward. For access to the three school districts that provided the basis for the original study, I want to thank Carl Cohn, Superintendent of Long Beach Unified School District, Marie MacArthur, Assistant to the Superintendent of the Cincinnati School District, and Alice Houston, Director of Human Resources for the Seattle Public Schools. These three individuals have significantly influenced my life as well as the context of this book. I also want to extend my thanks to the nine UCSC students who worked with me to gain a greater understanding of Asian American attitudes toward teachers and the teaching profession in the San Francisco Bay Area.

I am grateful to the editors and publishers of the Urban Review and the Journal of Teacher Education for publication of articles in which I draw from some of the research discussed in the present work.

My special appreciation goes to Andy Hargreaves and Ivor Goodson who believed that the research findings deserved a wider audience than that reached by previous journal articles. While John Ogbu and Barbara Gottesman were the first to suggest my writing the book, it was Hargreaves who literally brought the contract to the table. As editors for this series, Hargreaves and Goodson saw the relevance of the work and the need to move quickly into publication. Anna Clarkson at Falmer Press has been most able in facilitating this process.

Finally, I offer my thanks to William H. Heid for his support and encouragement. Throughout all the frustrations and time pressures, Bill has been able to provide our life with balance and sanity. It is to him that I dedicate this book. Without his assistance, it never would be yours to read.

June A. Gordon, Ph.D.
University of California, Santa Cruz
April 23, 1999

1   The Issues and the Research

Crisis in Urban Schools

No matter what one's orientation to public schooling in the United States, there appears to be a consensus that we need more teachers of color. The reasons include the increasingly low academic performance of students of color (Dentzer and Wheelock, 1990; Moore and Pachon, 1985); the inability and/or the unwillingness of middle-class teachers to teach low-income children of color (Book, Byers, and Freeman, 1983); the desire for communities of color to educate their own people (Hilliard, 1988); the need for all children to gain from a multiethnic teaching force (Banks and Banks, 1989); the high cost of prisons and welfare (Doston and Bolden, 1991); and the desire for a more honest representation in the curriculum of the diversity of ideas and skills that have contributed to the development of America (Gay, 1990). In addition, there are economic and world market competitive concerns that suggest the need to develop more adequately the human potential of all citizens (Sowell, 1983).

United States schools will have record enrollments of 52.7 million elementary and secondary students in the 1999 school year. Enrollment in public and private schools is 500,000 greater than in 1998. The United States Education Department projects that 2.2 million public school teachers must be hired in the next decade – both to replace those leaving the profession and to accommodate the growth in student population. According to Education Secretary Riley, the need for more teachers will pressure school districts to hire individuals who are not certified. Twenty-seven percent of newly hired teachers failed to meet state licensing requirements and nearly one-third of all teachers are teaching in a field they did not study as either a major or a minor subject in college. If hiring patterns remain as they are now, one-half to two-thirds of the millions of teachers hired in the next ten years will be first-time teachers.

Clearly, the shortage of teachers for urban youth verges on a national crisis. Although colleges of education continue to produce capable teachers, few of them are able or willing to work with the diversity demanded in urban school districts, regardless of their own ethnicity. Meeting the need for teachers who can understand the complexity of cultures that populate

1

our school yards is essential for both the children's success and our collective well-being. All communities must share the responsibility for ensuring the educational success of their youth, in part so that more of those youth will have the option of serving their communities as teachers. The knowledge required to educate the youth of today cannot be left to any one group or individual – we need the resources and skills of every community.

Although there is little research to demonstrate that an increase in teachers of color alone is sufficient to enhance academic achievement in students of color, there is evidence that a larger pool of teachers of color could make a difference in the futures of many minority children (King, 1993; Foster, 1997). The desire for an increase in minority participation in the teaching profession, however, is not based solely on the need for teachers of color to teach their own people; the demand for teachers of color in White communities is gaining momentum (Grant and Secada, 1989; Gifford, 1986). Many parents of today's generation of school children have finally come to realize that White children in homogenous schools face deficiencies in their education that could handicap their effective functioning in a multi-cultural world (Grant and Sleeter, 1989). Positive role models and the removal of stereotypes are as important for White children as for children of color. Teachers of color are pivotal in this awesome task of breaking down the centuries of misinformation and fear that have kept us separated and ignorant (Comer, 1988; Dilworth, 1992).

If the needs are apparently so great, then why the common perception that students of color are not interested in the field of teaching? The dominant view suggests that the resistance to selecting teaching as a career is because of low pay relative to other professions and increased alternative employment opportunities available to students of color (Robinson, 1981; Dupre, 1986). Although these may be reasons for some, they do not fully explain the lack of students of color in the profession. The choice to enter a profession, any profession, is influenced long before college by the perceptions and attitudes held within the families, communities and schools from which students emerge. Over the past twenty-five years as communities have become more fragmented because of job loss, increased mobility, and the fallout of desegregation, few working-class youth obtain their identities or images of career choice through contact with employed individuals within their communities (Aronowitz, 1992; Matute-Bianchi, 1991). Most young people are deluded by media images of unattainable success (Giroux, 1994). Simultaneously, many students are tracked into programs designed to reproduce the existing class structure based predominantly on socioeconomic conditions with outward manifestations of behavior, dialect, and dress. Bowles and Gintis (1976) set the stage for later critical theorists in insisting that occupational options are predetermined by hierarchical educational training. Historically, many students who were thus tracked into vocational programs lacked what Bourdieu and Passeron (1977) called 'cultural capital,' or skills and qualities associated with middle-class norms. Nevertheless, since working-class jobs were still available and respected, the lack of cultural capital in the sixties and seventies did not condemn one to a life of poverty (Sklar, 1995; W. Wilson, 1991; Aronowitz and Giroux, 1991). Working-class lives were not equated with poverty. Times have changed.

The issues related to increasing the participation of ethnic minority youth in teaching careers are nested and need to be seen in relationship rather than in isolation. The apparent reasons for low numbers of students of color entering the teaching profession vary among ethnic categories as well as within each category because of gender, immigrant status, regionalism, family educational and occupational background, as well as socioeconomic class. The proportion of college graduates entering teaching careers may be sufficiently high for African Americans, Latinos, and Native Americans but the absolute number is low due to lower rates of college completion. The research of Murnane and associates (Murnane, et al., 1991; Vegas, et al., 1998) suggests that we must distinguish between the total numbers of students choosing to teach and the proportion of students in each ethnic group so choosing. In some cases, the relative attractiveness of a career in teaching is less of an impediment than the lack of success in schooling that limits career options. Asian Americans offer a contrasting scenario of high rates of college completion but low interest in teaching.

The Need for Competent and Caring Teachers

One of the major educational concerns of our lifetime is the search for qualified and caring teachers for low-income immigrant and minority children who have become the majority population in American urban schools. My work is based on the premise that teachers of color are crucial contributors in their knowledge and number to the needs of urban schools. Teachers of color also provide an essential immediacy to the continuing multicultural education of fellow teachers. A more thorough understanding of the reasons why individuals of color do not choose the teaching profession should result in policies and programs designed to attract more students of color to the field. I argue that such an effort would also result in an improvement in teacher education programs training teachers to work in multicultural settings.

Although the need for teachers of color is embedded in a context of school desegregation, higher education elitism, racism, poverty, and urban decay, these societal and structural impediments cannot account fully for the resistance, hesitancy, or inability among students of color to pursue teaching as a career. What has not been discussed in previous work is how the images of professionalism and related cultural values of communities of color can undermine the aspirations of students of color who wish to enter teaching as a career. The most significant contribution of the research reported in this book comes in the form of opening up a new avenue for understanding low minority participation in teaching. Policies and programs in the past that have focused on structural and institutional barriers remain impotent without an understanding of the importance of history, culture, community attitudes, and expectations in shaping career choice, including the decision to embrace or eschew the teaching profession.

The distinctive qualities of one's ethnic community's experience and perception of schooling, past, present, and future, affect career decision making. How one perceives the impact of schooling on one's community and culture, how one is currently experiencing schooling, and how schooling is seen as a determinant in one's future options, all combine to develop an image of schooling and its professional practitioners. These attitudes, often based on stories and experiences passed down through families and communities, either encourage or discourage young people in their consideration of teaching as a career. As harmless, or as truthful, as these stories may be, they have a tremendous impact not only on a young person's view of education and their role in it as a student, but also on their willingness as a young adult to take on responsibility for the education of 'other people's children' (Delpit, 1995). This book suggests that the images of teachers and the teaching profession as developed and sustained within various American cultural and economic communities are as much a contribution to any shortage of teachers of color as are the structural impediments so frequently cited. If individuals have had negative educational experiences, and/or if they did not receive support or respect for their views while in school, they will have difficulty entertaining plans for a life-long occupation requiring their active participation and success in schooling. If parents or community members believed they were invalidated or misrepresented during their schooling they will not recommend teaching to their kin. If there is an assumption that participation in the perpetuation of public schooling not only undercuts one's cultural foundations but also removes one from the community, teaching will not be the vocation of choice.

Career choices for minorities grow out of common perceptions within minority families and communities. For reasons of immigrant experience and the racist nature of American culture, most non-White youth live much more within the authority of their elders than White middle-class youth living within the heralded modern culture of affluence and independence. Adult attitudes and guidance within communities of color carry a weight that rings a note of nostalgia in mainstream White America. The history of schooling as seen by communities of color and the resulting attitudes towards education provide a window through which we can view the causes for the apparent resistance of students of color towards entering the profession. This lens in turn provides valuable insights into how to prepare all students who choose teaching as a profession.

My position is that young people of color are, in reality, drawn to teaching and to other professions that promise to serve community needs as well as their own aspirations for economic and social mobility. Their path to such careers is impeded, however, by the quality of the schools they attend and the many influences upon life chances in a highly stratified and competitive 'free market' society that continues to practice racism as an everyday reality. To overcome such impediments, low-income and non-White youth need steady and clear encouragement to make the effort required to reach their professional goals. Given the accessibility and size of the profession, a possible career in teaching offers the most obvious source of motivation for academic effort among low-income students that opens the road to higher education and a choice of professions. The research presented in this book suggests that communities of color, including the teaching professionals thereof, are not providing the needed encouragement toward K-12 (Grades Kindergarten through Twelve of compulsory primary and secondary schools) teaching as one of those professional options.

The Image of Teaching

Perceptions of teaching as a profession have shifted over time. The attitudes exemplified by working-class students of color in urban schools are not the same as their parents or grandparents (Cummins, 1986). As education has moved from a privilege to a right, more and more students have come to see teachers in the role of laborers rather than professionals. Such a negative image of teaching was not present thirty years ago in the American South (Irvine, 1988; Siddle-Walker, 1993) nor is it a part of the baggage that immigrants bring to the US (Smith, 1994; Baruth and Manning, 1992). Although part of the process of identity formation in a country filled with immigrants is to adjust and modify one's behavior, expectations, and attitudes depending on the context, the cost has been extremely high (Rosaldo, 1989; Spindler, et al., 1990). I contend that negative attitudes towards teaching and a lack of respect for teachers among working-class communities of color have increased through greater contact with the values of middle-class White America.

The problem of lack of respect and negative image, therefore, seems to lie less with communities of color and more with the dominant society (Smith, 1994). Integrating into mainstream America means adapting to different attitudes and values, ones that focus on acquisition and individualism. As each group becomes more aware of the low status of teaching within the mainstream, adopted culture, they begin to take on those same attitudes. The teachers in this research contended that in order to survive in this 'society' you acquire the dominant stance, which in this case was to see teachers as less valuable than entrepreneurs. This process has assisted in the denigration of the teaching profession in the eyes of many teachers of color and their communities.

As Ogbu (1990) has noted numerous times, a 'crisis of confidence' in educational and economic institutions exists in many 'involuntary immigrant' communities. The crisis grows from communities of color questioning the relative benefits of public education for their children. Aware of the limitations on economic opportunity and of institutional racism, the community may not view schooling as an automatic avenue to economic and social success. They may, in fact, see their own economic deprivation as a result of a negative schooling experience. When teachers are perceived as the causes of their failure, it is unlikely that parents will encourage their children's aspirations for a career in teaching. Parents, adult kin, teachers, ministers, and community professionals are all potential sources of influence on minority youth regarding their future career choices (Zerfoss and Shapiro, 1974). If these individuals lose faith in the usefulness of public education in shaping future employment opportunities for their children, they will discourage and dissuade their youth from continuing in education as their life's profession (Reyhner, 1982).

The findings reported here suggest the need to question a developing consensus about teacher professionalism and a – 'one size fits all' – generic approach to the crisis in urban schools. Multiculturalism has been grafted on to a well-established form of professionalism that rests on standardized testing, scientific theories of learning, and the needs of a global economy for a newly skilled workforce (Gomez, 1993). The fit is awkward because the needs of urban communities struggling with racism, poverty, and declining levels of healthcare and other public services require more than superficial curricular reform. Greater numbers of teachers who are able to address the multiple demands of urban classrooms are one essential contribution. Those future teachers are now students in the very schools that need their dedication and skills. We must look beyond the addition of a multicultural approach to urban education if we are to prepare sufficient numbers and quality of teachers. I am suggesting a cyclical process that can spiral into despair with our diverse urban schools or can spiral toward success by addressing the impediments that urban students of color face on a path toward careers, including that of school teacher.

Historically, African American, Latino, Native American, and Asian American communities, each in their own way, have provided culturally specific schooling and culturally specific teachers in response to the European American majority's resistance to the inclusion of racially defined groups of fellow Americans within the common schools. The experience of these segregated schools was one of scarce resources and uncertain prospects for the children educated in them. Many of the teachers of these schools were members of the racial and cultural community within which the schools existed. Differences in class and educational resources between teacher and students were present but overridden by the racist context in which they were nested. Against the odds, segregated and isolated communities provided dignified schooling for their children while generations of educators served their communities with mutual respect.

Over the past fifty years, American society has gradually dismantled segregated schooling as a legal and professional institution. The continuing facts of segregated schooling, however, contradict that effort. Urban schools attended largely by racial minority and poor children have increased during the past twenty years (Orfield, 1994). It is here where the need for new teachers is greatest. If teacher education and related public policy are to respond to this need, the 'color of teaching' must be addressed. My work suggests that such a response must combine preparation of all new teachers for the distinctive challenges of urban schools along with the recruitment of teachers from communities of color. People of color are an essential source of teachers who are responsive to the needs of students of color. They also constitute the actual supply of educated individuals who will be available as teachers in the coming generations.

In a variety of scenarios that follow, spanning four ethnic groups, I show how the nature of demands for greater representation and voice in the education of minority youth paradoxically coexist with resistance to encouraging such youth to enter the field of teaching. It is this tension that needs to be understood if we are ever to create an honest dialogue about how we can best educate all children. A discussion of the historical context of segregation, exclusion, and immigration provides a backdrop for understanding the responses by the four ethnic groups covered in this study. Emphasis is given to the value placed on teaching and sacrifices made during times when education was restricted or outlawed. The role of schooling versus education and what is lost with formal schooling are presented from the vantage point of traditional societies. This history has clearly influenced the views that the teachers and other informants hold towards public school education and its teachers as shared in the interviews reported here.

Although much ethnic group research is limited to one group (Deyhle, 1992; Keefe and Padilla, 1987; Stack, 1974; Duran, 1983; J. King, 1994; Gandara, 1995; Foster, 1994), I reason that there are important issues to be confronted that can only be heard when spoken by a variety of voices. The research that most approximates to this approach is that of John Ogbu. Beginning in the early 1970s, Ogbu went into several communities of color, mostly Latino and African American, in Stockton, California, to inquire into individuals' perceptions of schooling and education (Ogbu, 1974). His more recent research, focused on the San Francisco area, includes a third major group, Asian Americans. Thus far, Ogbu's findings demonstrate the complexity and variation within and between racial groups, depending on a wide range of factors that we often refuse to acknowledge in our simplistic attempt to categorize along racial lines (Ogbu and Simons, 1998).

The language of color

Throughout this work, the notion of a community of color is in question. Why are there such communities in United States society? What is the history that explains their existence and the quality of life available within these communities? I have chosen to use racial identity in my work both for the convenience of matching the contemporary usage and to emphasize the essentially racist nature of the process. United States culture is founded on racial thinking that assumes the inferiority of peoples who have been stigmatized through lives of slavery and conquest and who can be physically identified within the racial practices of mainstream society. The risk of over-generalizing when dealing with any one of the four major non-White racial categories in United States demography is great; the risks when working with all four are extreme.

A related issue is that not all members of any of these groups have lived within an intact racial community. Urban life in America has never been strictly segregated and economic differences often complicate racial community distinctions. When the issue of immigration is added to our analysis, the situation is both clearer in terms of a 'home community' and more complicated by how American society has variously welcomed its newer, late twentieth-century immigrants (Rumbaut, 1995; Shorris, 1992). The present work narrows the focus by relying on America's official racial categories rather than the complexity of immigrant origins. In fact, the large number of immigrants from the many cultures of Asia and South and Central America has redefined the perceptions of urban schooling; and the historically constructed racial categories of American society are once more undergoing transformation.

In this study the term 'teacher of color' includes individuals who are self-identified and so accepted by their employing school district as belonging to one of four ethnic categories used for official reporting: Latino/Hispanic, African American/Black, Asian American, and Native American. The actual variety of identities is much more complex and interesting as is occasionally made explicit in the text. The terminology of color is as varied in my writing as it is in common usage. I made no attempt to standardize my usage or in any way alter the language of those interviewed, Black is interchangeable with African American, with some recognition for the complexity of Puerto-Rican, Cuban, and other Afro-Caribbean identities that overlap with Latino or Hispanic identities. The term Indian still has currency among Native Americans and both terms attempt to include several hundred distinct and indigenous cultures of the Americas. Latino has been favored in my work over the official term, Hispanic, and includes the various identities of native and immigrant peoples with Mexican, Central and South American ancestry, including Cubans and Puerto Ricans. Asian American is truly a mixed category and for my work is restricted to the peoples of East and Southeast Asia. Gibson's work with Punjabi students in California (1988) is a powerful reminder of the actual diversity within America's Asian peoples. The Pilipino identity represents a blend of Latino and Asian categories and I have chosen to follow the customary practice and include them within the Asian American identity. Within America's racist traditions, color is a genuine basis for life chances. Thus, the terms 'student of color' and 'teacher of color' are not just terms of convenience but the result of peoples of many cultures having been subject to redefinition within a racialized multiethnic culture (Omi and Winant, 1986; Smedley, 1999).

The Research Process

I began this research assuming that the main causes for the low number of students of color entering the field of teaching had to do with social and institutional impediments. These views had been substantiated by my prior research on minority culture-based student programs at six college campuses in the state of Washington (Gordon, 1997a). That work explored the impediments that *college* students of color face in their access to, and success in, predominantly White institutions of higher education. The findings convinced me that the crucial difficulties lay not with college life but with life prior to college, especially academic preparation and socialization toward career choice. If students were not adequately prepared for higher education, in both of these areas, they were less likely to persist toward professional careers, including that of school teacher. I realized that if I were to understand access and retention issues for students of color in higher education I had to look at pre-collegiate experiences.

Based on the assumption that knowledge of, and interest in, a profession often comes from what people hear and see most frequently, I began a study in 1991 of attitudes towards teaching among approximately sixty individuals who were professionally involved with youth in the Seattle area. The purpose of this study was to identify which particular group of individuals and which questions could best illuminate the issues behind the shortage of teachers of color. As a criterion for selection I looked for people who had expertise in the area of minority student career choice and teaching careers in particular. The panel included university faculty members and administrators, school teachers, graduate students, counselors, and community workers from a variety of ethnic groups: African American, Latino, Asian American, Native American, and European American. Most were people of color. Through the use of open-ended interviewing, informants were asked to expound on the question: 'Why do you think students of color are not selecting teaching as a career?' At the end of four months of interviews, I organized and summarized the perceptions of the panel as part of a critical understanding of the impediments and inducements facing non-White youth in their choice of teaching as a career (Gordon, 1997b).

Although nearly all informants mentioned greater economic incentives as important in attracting and retaining teachers of color, money was *not* the pivotal reason students were resisting teaching as a career. Most informants of color believed that the main reason students of color reject teaching as a career is the negative experience they have had in school. A few commented that students had little desire to return to an environment that they consider racist and that inhibited their access to an adequate education. The informants were overwhelmingly preoccupied with the quality of schooling given to kids of color, respect for decision-making capabilities within communities of color, and the need for support from institutions of higher education. They spoke of the need for curricular and institutional change that would reflect the diversity of cultures and learning styles represented in our schools. There was a continuing sense, given the strength of commitment among communities of color to education and the history of that commitment in the face of obstacles, that more students of color would choose to teach if they experienced more support and encouragement for academic success as well as stronger preparation for college and professional careers.

From this preliminary study, it became clear that school teachers played a significant role in their students' perceptions of education and, hence, of teaching as a profession. How well teachers were prepared to teach diverse students and interact with students' families and communities appeared to be a crucial factor in altering the current shortage of teachers of color. The results overall led me to conclude that persons of color who had experienced the whole process of influence and schooling to the point of choosing to teach would be the best informants for further research on students of color and their choice to enter teaching as a profession; they had not only succeeded academically but had chosen education as their life's work. Most of them were probably teaching students of color in urban schools and had a sense of how both students and parents viewed them as teachers as well as the teaching profession overall.

Three urban school districts and their teachers of color

As a result of the preliminary study, I sought to both narrow the pool of informants and broaden the geographic area in which they resided in order to demonstrate the power and diversity of views within what we have come to call 'people of color' or 'minorities.' By narrowing the choice of informants to teachers of color, I hoped to avoid the accusation that views in conflict with popular myths or beliefs could be attributed to the 'dominant' culture. I further wanted to explore the similarities and differences between and within the arbitrarily defined 'ethnic groups' of Latino/Hispanic, African American/Black, Asian American, and Native American/Indian. I decided to look at schools in three major urban communities that represented radically different migration patterns and, hence, orientation to public education. Over a period of two years I visited several schools each in Seattle, Washington, Long Beach, California, and Cincinnati, Ohio and conducted 116 interviews with teachers of color. Given their personal experience of schooling and the history of schooling in their communities, I sought to find out from these teachers what they had to say about students of color and the choice of a career in teaching.

My access to each of these school districts began long before the research project was conceived. Based on relationships that I had cultivated with members of the community and on prior contacts with the administration, I had developed a reputation for trust and unobtrusiveness. People knew my background and supported my work. Perhaps most important, I had stayed in contact with 'the community.' In each of these three urban school districts I knew someone who could assist me in gaining access to the teachers of the district. In all three cases the contact happened to be an African American administrator. In one case it was the superintendent, in another, a member of the district administration, and, in the third, the Director of Human Resources. The choice of schools to be used in the study for each district was determined by these individuals based on guidelines that I provided: a balance between teachers of all four ethnic groups mentioned above; geographic variation within the city; economic variation among the schools; and schools from all grade levels: high school, middle, and elementary.

All of the schools visited in the three cities are considered 'inner city,' with both a preponderance of students of color and their 'quota' of teachers of color. In each district all three levels of schools, elementary, middle, and high school, were represented. They ranged from elite 'Latin prep' to 'project' schools as well as 'alternative' schools that work with special populations. Some of these alternatives are defined along ethnic lines; others on academic terms such as vocational schools; and still others are thematically delineated such as academies for 'the basics' or the arts. The 'ethnocentric' programs included a Native American school that had been developed for and by Native people and alternative programs for African American youth who had received multiple suspensions and expulsions.

Out of the four major ethnic groups represented by the teachers interviewed in Seattle, Cincinnati, and Long Beach, only twenty of the informants were Asian American, a reflection of their low participation in the teaching force. In order to gain a better understanding of this scarcity, I gathered another fifty interviews from individuals of Asian identity in the San Francisco region. The informants included staff at a bilingual Chinese program for newly arrived immigrants as well as students, professionals, and family members of my students. Interviews with members of the community who were not teachers provided an alternative lens in understanding how attitudes towards the profession are developed and transmitted to youth. All of the informants interviewed were called on to address the issue of recruitment and preparation of teachers to work in predominately low-income, non-White, and immigrant schools and reflect on the challenges of recruiting and preparing students of color for urban classrooms.

The sites

Cincinnati sits along the northern bank of the Ohio River, the traditional boundary of North and South in the American Midwest, but reflects much of Southern American culture. The school population is basically 'Black/White' with sixty-three percent of the students African American, thirty-five percent White, predominantly Appalachian or Southern mountain heritage, less than one percent Asian, and one percent 'other.' Most of the teachers had been raised in Southeastern states and carried Southern values and attitudes. Some teachers in Cincinnati were unaware that 'minority' denoted anything other than African American.

Seattle, far to the Northwest and clearly on the 'Pacific Rim,' in contrast to Cincinnati, is considered 'integrated.' This was usually translated as meaning the schools have a balance between Asian American, African American, Native American and White students. Most of the informants raised in the Seattle schools were proud of having had friends from a range of ethnicities. Current percentages for the school district overall continue to reflect this balance: African American, twenty-four percent, White, forty-three percent, Asian American, twenty-three percent, Hispanic, seven percent, and Native American, three percent.

Among the cities I visited, Long Beach has the largest proportion of non-White students. At present, African Americans make up eighteen percent of the school age population, White, twenty-five percent, Asian American, seventeen percent, Latino, thirty-four percent, Pilipino, three percent, Pacific Islander, two percent, and one percent Native American. The Long Beach schools are further distinguished by the linguistic diversity that is added to the cultural and economic diversity of the students. At the middle school level, some schools have as many as sixty percent LEP, limited English proficiency, students. In the high schools this drops to around thirty percent, mostly because of the soaring drop-out rate of LEP students. Economic disadvantage similarly strikes Long Beach the hardest. Eleven out of the fifteen middle schools have more than fifty percent 'economically disadvantaged' students, one is as high as eighty-eight percent. High schools fare a little better, but not much.

Similarly, when looking at the teaching staff for the three districts, a different picture emerges for each. Cincinnati with its sixty-three percent African American student population has forty percent of its staff African American. Seattle with fifty-seven percent minority students, has twenty-three percent teachers of color. Long Beach, with the largest minority school age population of seventy-five percent has the lowest percentage of teachers of color, twenty-one percent. Given the significant differences between the numbers of teachers of color in the three districts and my attempt to interview approximately the same number of teachers of color in each district, the teachers of color interviewed as a percentage of the total varied considerably. In Cincinnati, it was four percent, all African American. In Seattle, it was seven percent and in Long Beach it was six percent. Both Seattle and Long Beach offered representation from all ethnic groups, while Long Beach had more Latino interviewees and Seattle had more Asian and Native American.

Although all three of the school systems are urban, the migratory patterns of their non-White teacher populations vary greatly, particularly the African Americans. Most of the older African American teachers in Seattle had been brought from the South to Seattle under a special recruitment effort in the early 1970s in an attempt to diversify the teaching force. There was considerable upset regarding this outside recruitment as Seattle at that time had a sizeable and educated African American population from which to draw. Even to this day there is tension and angst between the African Americans who had been 'brought in' and those who were 'residents' at the time and were excluded from the pool of original hires twenty-five years ago. The recruited teachers self-identified as Southerner and noted that their current values were clearly shaped more by their Southern upbringing than the Seattle context.

Long Beach has historically been an important port of entry for immigrants from all parts of the world as well as African Americans and Whites migrating from the US South. Most of the African American teachers in Long Beach came as part of a general migration of Blacks and Whites before and during World War II in search of work in the naval shipyards and aircraft factories. Some of their offspring provided the pool of African American teachers currently in the system. Few members of this latter group self-identified as Southern. Some of them identified as mixed race, many of them are middle to upper-middle class, well traveled, and well educated. Several had held other professional jobs. These characteristics held true for many of the Asian, Latino, and Native American teachers in Long Beach as well. Given its proximity to the US-Mexican border, there has always been a strong Latino presence. Most recently, immigration has swelled from Central America, Southeast Asia, the Pacific Islands, and Eastern Europe.

As mentioned earlier, the interviews in Cincinnati were all with African American teachers, the vast majority identifying with their Southern heritage. The issue was not so much migration as movement into urban centers. Cincinnati, as one of the starting points for the underground railroad for escaping slaves and an urban center for a large rural region, remains tied psychologically to its roots, both for Appalachian Whites and Southern Blacks. Only the youngest informants, those under 35 years of age, made no mention of the South; two of these teachers were clearly mixed race. It is interesting that only in Cincinnati, where all teachers interviewed identified as African American, did two teachers (not those who were mixed race) note their sexual orientation as an important factor in providing diversity to the district. Although there may have been other teachers in the study in Seattle and Long Beach who are gay or lesbian, no others had openly so identified.

The teacher informants were categorized and are identified in the book according to their dominant non-White identity by a code that combines their ethnic identity and gender, e.g. (LAm) for a Latino male, (AFf) for an African American female, (NAm) for a Native American male and (ASf) for an Asian American female. The actual variety is much greater. There were teachers of mixed race who referred to themselves as mulatto or Creole and stressed the importance of the values of both parents in determining their career choice and academic success. Still, even these individuals self-identified with one of the four standard categories. The informants were from different age groups and were educated and given teacher training in different parts of the country at different points in time. Although most received a public education, some were educated in private schools. African Americans who were raised in the South and Mexican Americans who came from some of the Southwestern states would be expected to have different views from those individuals who have not participated in a segregated educational and social system. Some were first-generation college students, others were from families with several generations of higher education.

The researcher

A variable in any research is the interviewer. As an individual, I come to this work after many years of experience in communities of color with people from diverse backgrounds in the United States and other countries. As a scholar, I have conducted previous research and writing in related topics using open-ended interviewing techniques with notable success. Being raised in an inner city where I attended multiracial, multilingual public schools helped increase my awareness of the lives of the students within the schools I interviewed. I was raised in a lower-income, immigrant, working-class family by British parents who refused to assimilate into American society. A gift resulting from this upbringing is an acute awareness of differences in class, race, and language. My youth also provided me with the ability to develop trust quickly with most people, regardless of their orientation. Trust provides the basis for establishing a sense of integrity and honesty in the interviews for this research. The fact that I have lived in a variety of cultures and am able to speak several languages has enabled me to break through many of the walls of fear that often surround those who have not been able to participate in the larger conversations of communities foreign to their experience. I have been fortunate over the years to connect with a range of individuals who have given me access to their communities, their schools, their hopes and their dreams. This book, in part, shares their perceptions of their past, present, and future in terms of understanding the shortage of teachers of color in the profession.

Communities of Color and the Teaching Profession

Each of the next four chapters begins with a discussion of the historical context for how a specific community of color has experienced and participated in schooling through the teaching profession. The historical context sets the stage for each community's views on how the image of teaching as a profession has changed during the past twenty to thirty years as separate and segregated schooling evolved into legally integrated but often still unequal education. For each community of color, I present the perspectives offered in the interviews on the question of why students of color do or do not choose teaching as a career. All four chapters in Part II conclude with the question of whether students of color are encouraged to enter the teaching profession.

Within the overall issue of encouragement, I wanted to know if these teachers of color ever recommended teaching as a career to their own students or children. It is from this flow of inquiry that I came across the most devastating finding of the study: teachers of color, parents, and community members tend *not* to encourage their youth to enter the field of teaching. The theme of discouragement rang through not only the interviews with teachers of color in the national study but also in the other research projects mentioned in this book, conducted with college students of color and community members. It is ironic that, while the need for more teachers of color increases, encouragement decreases.

Some individuals were actually embarrassed by the question, 'Do you recommend teaching to your students or family?' particularly if in answering an earlier question they had revealed their anger or frustration with the profession, the students, and the state of their own children's education. Although some of their personal stories reflected their own youthful disdain for schooling, many of the teachers were unwilling to cut much slack for the youth of today, convinced that most young people are materialistic and media-driven. Their standards for the profession remained exceedingly high even though some of them had come into teaching through very precarious channels with minimal qualifications. These views need to be understood in light of the historical context of each racial group and the differences in socioeconomic class between many of the students who were low income and most of the teachers who came from middle-class backgrounds. Some teachers believed that only the most capable should be recommended to teach while others thought that teaching had less to do with intelligence than it does with caring and helping. Still others saw leadership and inquisitiveness as essential ingredients. The responses reflect some of this confusion. Given the respect and reverence that most traditional societies place on elders, to be told by an adult member of your community that you are either incapable of becoming a teacher or that teaching is beneath you, leaves an indelible mark. By assuming that becoming a teacher is not good enough for our children on the one hand, or that the profession is too demanding on the other, we abrogate our responsibility and therefore endanger our future. If teachers who work with urban youth and who have selected teaching themselves as their life profession are not recommending teaching as a career path, then who will?

The Historical Context

Within the various non-White communities across the United States, education has traditionally been held in high esteem. The unwillingness of White society in the United States to support the non-White minority communities in the education of their own people brought about neglect, deprivation, and unequal segregation. With desegregation came a new form of separation as those who assimilate are rewarded and those that do not are differentially educated or pushed out of the system, often as a result of their resistance to mainstream schooling. Throughout the interviews presented in this book, you will perhaps be surprised by the many stories that allude to the days before and during early desegregation of United States schools, a process that has continued with mixed success since the 1950s. Some of the voices reflect on what it was like to be the first 'minority' teacher in their districts. Others relate how it felt to move from working with a homogenous group of students sharing a common set of cultural traditions and way of viewing the world to working with kids from various backgrounds. Interestingly, some of the same conflicts arose for Asian Americans as for African Americans, Latinos, and Native Americans. All of these peoples have rich traditions where education and teachers are held in high esteem.

Some of the teachers interviewed, especially the younger ones, have embraced integration as it creates opportunities to revision themselves and move into areas previously unavailable. Seeing the preservation of culture as conservative and confining, their movement into mainstream society and beyond the historical demarcation lines has meant breaking with the past and its folkways, a liberation from constraints of tradition. Others see integration as dissolution, blending without distinction, loss without gain. For most, school integration has been a mixed blessing for communities of color. Although desegregation has provided opportunities heretofore unknown, it has also served as a way of diluting the strength of ethnic communities, which had been previously defined and circumscribed by racial discrimination, *de jure* and *de facto*. Ironically, some of the greatest losses to these communities were in education, the backbone of any culture.

How each of the teachers interviewed has chosen to negotiate the turbulent waters of United States ethnic group relations depends on many factors, including time away from 'home culture,' whether this be Mexico, China, the reservation, or 'the South,' and the social and cultural capital that encompasses socioeconomic class, parents' education and expectations, and access to educational resources. I will first address the situation for African Americans and then the parallel scenario that holds true for Native Americans and Mexican Americans. Asian Americans provide a quite different story.

2   African American Teachers

The Changing Historical Context for African American Teachers

Education took place on slave plantations long before it was legal or profitable for African Americans to be taught to read. Small, 'illegal schools' for African Americans existed for years without being discovered. These were mainly run by Black women who had gained some education and secretly passed it on to fellow slaves (Perkins, 1989). Anderson (1988), discussing this commitment to education from an historical perspective, explains how ex-slaves played a central role in the idea of public education. Education, however, was severely curtailed to conform to the needs for cheap and docile labor in an increasingly low-skilled approach to cotton production. In the Northern states during the slavery era, educated African Americans mingled relatively freely with Whites and worked in a wide variety of skilled occupations and professions (Horton and Horton, 1979). Many of the most privileged African Americans, the so-called 'Black bourgeoisie,' who were often light-skinned as well as financially secure, wanted their children educated with Whites and were pro-integration in all facets of society (W. Banks, 1996). In contrast, the Black middle class, often of mixed heritage and more tenuous economic condition, were somewhat ostracized from elite circles and preferred that their children be educated within their own communities (Birmingham, 1977). It is this latter group that then formed the backbone of the teaching force for Black schools. Teaching as a profession became a self-perpetuating affair with certain families grooming their own to take over. These individuals had a great deal invested in teaching. The Black middle class were opposed to integration, believing that segregated schooling provided them with the opportunity to demonstrate to Whites that African Americans could provide an equal and adequate education for their own people. It further allowed them to instill values in their youth that were lacking in the White community; moreover, it insured some of them a professional position (Perkins, 1989).

Because of the limited opportunities available to African Americans in the South and the constraints placed on Whites teaching Black children, many African Americans, who under a more just system might have gone into other professions, worked as teachers. In 1950, teaching accounted for nearly half of Black professional workers, compared to less than one quarter of White professionals (Cole, 1986). The lack of access to other professions, ironically, increased the competence and qualifications of Black teachers (Siddle-Walker, 1993). It was not unusual for Black teachers to have more formal education than the White teachers who later replaced them after desegregation. As the economic condition of Southern Black Americans continued to deteriorate during the overall hardship of the 1930s, so did the conditions in the segregated Black schools. Unable to attract funding or assistance, a plea went out for integration of public schooling based on the hope that with White involvement would come more resources (Sowell, 1983). What was not anticipated was the degree to which this would affect the jobs held by Black teachers and principals.

When school desegregation arrived, many White parents did not want their children educated by Black teachers (Dougherty, 1998). If White children were now going to be in the room they must have White teachers, even if there were more Black children present (Philipsen, 1994). Thousands of Black teachers lost their jobs with integration; but, more importantly, the Black community lost leaders and children lost their role models and guides (Sizemore, 1986). This came at a time when there was a dramatic increase of Black children in the school system. Many educated Black men and women who had once served their community were now unemployed. By the time the court and federal actions were initiated in the late 1960s and 1970s to prevent further displacements, the damage had already been done. Schooling became a part of the White man's world; education was undermined, taken from the community and placed in the hands of others. White teachers who knew little, if anything, about the education of Black children arrived ill prepared and ill informed (Peshkin, 1992). It is not that desegregation was designed to neglect Black culture but rather, that many of those who came and continue to teach African American youth have had little understanding of or respect for African American history or community context. As a result, desegregation unleashed a distrust of an educational system over which the Black community no longer held sway (Foster, 1994).

Since teaching in the Black community had traditionally remained in the hands of a relatively small middle class, once these individuals chose or were forced to move into mainstream society to use their talents, they did so, leaving a shortage of teachers. The loss of these educators accentuated the gap that has existed for years between middle-class and lower-class African Americans. It also left many urban communities with fewer educated role models. This void in the Black community continues today and some would say it is the primary cause of the low academic success of inner city youth. There has long been a fear on the part of African American parents that their children would not receive 'fair' treatment, that Whites would not provide the structure or discipline to which their children were accustomed, and that Whites would have lower expectations for Black students (Delpit, 1988).

Many of the teachers I interviewed believed that with desegregation came the loss of control by the Black community over the education, and hence the future, of Black youth. The perception holds that many White teachers are generally unprepared to teach students in urban schools effectively, resulting in internal segregation in the form of tracking, special classes, differential drop-out rates and a continuing advantage for middle-class White students. The process has continued now for three generations with only gradual changes. The results of this history surface in a combination of inadequate academic success and negative attitudes toward schooling among many members of communities of color and a teaching profession that has been chronically ineffective in communities of color. It is this interplay of history, current reality, and possible future options that affects the image of teachers and respect for the profession. In the following section we see how these attitudes have changed over the years and the power of their influence as folk wisdom on the career decisions of African American youth.

African American Teachers Speak to the Image of Teaching

Many of the ideas that the African American teachers expressed in interviews about the status and image of teachers were based on the African American experience in the South from the Post-Reconstruction 1880s to the 1950s, when teaching in segregated schools was one of the few professions that Blacks could enter and when teaching was viewed as the most productive way to bring about the 'uplift of the race' (Gaines, 1996; Morris, et al., 1998). Teaching in Black communities was elevated to a level of respect unparalleled in mainstream American society. Because of the stature that African American teachers had in the South, they became community leaders, setting standards for appropriate language, behavior, and dress (Comer, 1988; McCullough-Garrett, 1993). The interviews reported here suggest that, because of this history, African American teachers feel the stigma of low esteem for their profession far greater than any other racial group, including Whites.

One result of desegregation was the withdrawal of the Black community from active participation in public schooling. For teachers who remained in the field, desegregation meant participating in a larger society, one which did not hold their profession in high esteem (Adair, 1984). Ironically then, integration coincided with a decrease in respect for teaching as a profession. This is not to be confused with a lack of respect towards Black teachers in the Black community. Rather, the contention expressed in the interviews was that African American teachers are respected within their community but not among mainstream society. Within the community, teachers are still seen as an educated elite bringing hope and possibility to young people's lives.

About one half of all African Americans interviewed identified as Southern and spoke kindly, if not proudly, of the 'South.' They reflected fondly on the benefits of a separate education system whose teachers were held in high esteem and which provided them with the confidence and survival skills that have enabled them to succeed in life:

> Teachers were looked on differently in the South; they were highly respected. Jobs were viewed as careers then. Doctors, ministers, and teachers, you never argued with them; they had you covered. The smaller the community, the more true. Yes, it was a different world in the South. The things that inspired me to go into teaching aren't there now. Qualities and character were different. The expectations were high. They inspired us to learn; they wanted me to get the basics; the information was relevant. They dressed professional. Now the manner and motivation are gone. You can't have teachers wearing jeans. A chaotic environment is not conducive to learning.
>
> (80/AFm)

Clearly the concern with manner and style shared importance with content, giving the profession an air of dignity not often found today. Such concern also supports the importance of caring and other affective qualities that the teachers throughout the interviews saw as extremely important. The deviation from this sense of propriety was seen by many African Americans as the source of the decline in the status of teachers and in schooling itself. Several teachers explained the logic behind this attitude: 'The perception of teacher comes from appearance, enthusiasm, sincerity, neatness. We should dress for success.' (40/AFf) 'The way teachers carry themselves does not engender an interest in teaching.' (80/AFm)

Confusion over the role and demeanor of teachers is a significant side-effect of desegregation. Many African American teachers expect a higher degree of control, structure, and respect than their White counterparts. The less structured, more relaxed approach to teaching taken by many mainstream teachers often irritates those raised with Southern manners and memories. The perception remains that teachers who care about their students also care about how they present themselves: 'I had an outstanding preparation [in teacher education in the South]. We were told how to stay attractive, maintain a neat classroom, be a symbol of hope. They taught us how to care and love. This was transmitted to the kids.' (26/AFf)

The recurring complaint throughout my conversations with African American teachers that 'teaching isn't glamorous anymore' (74/AFf) fascinated me. The idea was not regional, but it did seem to be cultural. It is noteworthy that no other group, Latinos, Native Americans or Asians, mentioned this as a consideration for their people even though, in comparison to White teachers, most of the teachers of color in all ethnic groups were far better dressed. Comments such as: 'Teaching is not viewed as a profession that is exciting and glamorous, [so it] doesn't attract youth' (15/AFm) and, 'It's not as glamorous as engineering. You don't hear fabulous things about teachers anymore' (11/AFf), highlighted this issue. Middle-aged African American teachers were the most likely to comment on the fact that teachers should be treated the same as doctors and lawyers:

> In my parents' background [the South], teachers were up there with doctors and lawyers. Especially as one of few opportunities for Black women. Now teaching is different; I feel like a common laborer. In the West, teaching is not glamorous. You're subject to unionization and strikes like everyone else.
>
> (16/AFf)

Although the comfortable majority of educators may take this concern with appearance as insubstantial, in a capitalist society how one displays wealth, especially in low-income areas, can be of great significance, especially when students only see their teachers within the context of school. For children from working-class families, a teacher is often the only professional with whom they associate on a regular basis. With regard to attracting students of color to the field of teaching, these teachers argued that students make judgments about careers based on what they 'see' in terms of clothes, car, jewelry, etc. When teachers drive old cars or dress in sweats, students assume that teachers cannot afford anything better. As indicated in these two comments: 'Educators don't present themselves; they dress down, drive old cars. Kids see what is immediately visible, status.' (10/AFm)

> It started in the 70s when teachers started wearing T-shirts and jeans and teachers treated students like peers. This is the cause of the loss of respect. I tell kids to dress for success, but teachers don't do it. They [students] see a connection between what they [teachers] wear and what they [teachers] earn.
>
> (78/AFf)

Since few teachers live in the community in which they teach, especially the inner city, this conjecture is not so far out of line (Sizemore, 1986). In contrast to life in the South, students in urban communities seldom see their teachers at church, at the grocery store, or around their homes. What occurs in the classroom is all students have to go on. As an aside, it is interesting to note that many mainstream teachers say that they drive old cars and 'dress down' so that they can better relate to their low-income students. The assumption is that they do not want to stand apart from their students; they want to gain their trust and confidence and assume that by de-emphasizing hierarchy as seen through status and displays of wealth, they will be more easily accepted. This is not how these African American teachers saw it.

Several teachers acknowledged the changes in values in the modern youth of today claiming that 'Instant gratification is the main concern for Blacks.' (40/AFf, 37/AFm, 43/AFf) Others despaired at young people's inability to move beyond selfish needs toward service to the community. Some teachers, although understanding that 'glamour' is what kids buy into, did not support the idea themselves and actually saw the perpetuation of this need as dangerous. The excessive interest in immediate gratification demonstrated by today's youth was foreign to some of the teachers. A mixed-race male teacher explained:

> The redirection of the entire culture places the emphasis on monetary gains versus the JFK image that I grew up with. In my age group (fortyish) we had a consciousness that is different from today's. Students are now more disoriented; the family is fragmented.
>
> (15/AFm)

Further exceptions to the African American focus on image came from those teachers who were second- and third-generation professionals and/or who had tried other careers before coming into teaching. One older male teacher offered perspective and hope: 'Historically, teaching has been an esteemed profession for Blacks. This has been eroded. But in the last five years there has been a reversal in this. People are beginning to see how important teaching is to their children's future.' (17/AFm) Still there were those who questioned whether the damage done to the teaching profession had left it unsuitable for African Americans to enter. As one teacher said: 'Teaching is just not attractive to Blacks as a profession.' (3/AFf)

African American Teachers' Perceptions of Why Students of Color Resist Teaching as a Profession

When asked to discuss whether or not students of color resist teaching as a profession, African American teachers generally agreed that students in their schools and communities did not consider teaching a viable or attractive career choice. The reasons given by the teachers have been arranged into three broad categories: economic, educational, social/cultural. Economic reasons focused on low pay, too much education for the return, and a wider range of career choices than for previous generations of African Americans. Educational reasons included inadequate K-12 schooling, negative school experiences, and lack of support in college. Social/cultural reasons centered on racism, lack of encouragement, and racelessness.

Economic reasons: Low pay

The most automatic and immediate response that comes to the question, 'Why do *you* think students of color are not going into the field of teaching?' is that the pay is too low. Although I can understand this assumption coming from the general populace who remain relatively unaware of the actual pay structure of most jobs, including teaching, I was amazed at how many of the informants shot out this response. Usually the comments came without explanation or context. It was as if this was a given, an obvious fact of which any intelligent person would be aware. Most of the teachers who claimed pay as the main impediment simply used words such as 'not enough money,' 'low pay,' or 'income' when answering the question, as if the meaning was understood and the concern shared. The significance of pay, however, in the career decision-making process varied greatly. As excerpts from the interviews show, the variation in meaning of economic worth is great and is often conflated with an individual's perception of self-worth. Culture and history played a major role in influencing teachers' attitudes towards money. Confusion pervaded the conversations when we discussed attitudes of professionalism and why some jobs are rewarded more than others.

African Americans, in particular, believed that teachers were underpaid. Comments such as 'What we get is not enough money when compared to doctors and lawyers' (68/AFf) and 'We should get the same money as a doctor. We have to get almost as much education and we are dealing with human beings!' (11/AFf) reflect some of the misunderstandings mentioned above. The educational requirements for these professions are radically different. Type and choice of clientele also powerfully affect one's status and income. Children's needs have historically been perceived as appropriate for non-professional service and mostly unpaid female service as well. Public school teachers work for the government; you cannot set your own salary scale. Government jobs, being stable and secure, tend not to reward performance but rather time of service. This is as true for university professors as it is for K-12 teachers. All of these factors, however unjustified, contribute to the limited salaries of schoolteachers when compared with the well-paid professionals who provide the image of success in America.

Even though low pay was the most immediate reason given by more than half of the teachers for students of color's resistance to teaching careers, most of the more thoughtful responses actually countered this prevailing view. Reflecting on how the image of teachers' pay may have been formed, one teacher noted how the union has been forced into an awkward position requiring it to advocate higher wages at the expense of portraying teachers as paupers.

> I don't think that money is the real issue. It's a myth. The union is working against us. By advocating for more income for teachers, they

give a bad image of the profession. It's an irony. They have to say that we are poorly paid in order to get more money, but then, everyone thinks that it's [teaching] a low-paying job.

(53/AFf)

Others often mentioned the *benefits of teaching* in their arguments. One teacher elaborated on this topic at length:

Teachers actually have more stability than business. After three years, they have tenure – have a job for the rest of your life, even with five years off or whatever. Monetary-wise, teachers may look underpaid, but we have ten automatic sick days and lots of benefits. If we choose to go into another type of business, you have enough time in the day to do this. Big business doesn't care about family. Education is all about children and is a more understanding employer. Education works around your children.

(19/AFf)

It is important to note the power of socioeconomic class in shaping attitudes towards income. Those teachers who were from professional families held radically different views on the importance of money in relation to teaching and on jobs of comparable worth. Two interviews stand out vividly. One African American woman related to me the story of her siblings' employment patterns:

My family are all professionals. My brother is an accountant, my sister-in-law is a nurse, and my older brother is a banking executive. All of us receive comparable wages, but they have to work longer hours; they work weekends and are on-call. We [teachers] don't; I'm out of here by four o'clock.

(78/AFf)

Although the above comment came from a female teacher, some of the men were equally attracted to teaching not just because of the stability and autonomy it provided in comparison to business but because it provided them with a way to assist others. These views are reflected in a few of the powerful comments that follow: 'You can't put monetary value on self-worth. Education must be viewed not by material gains received but by the improvement of their well-being, regardless of socioeconomic status. Money can't be the issue with any profession' (15/AFm); 'You won't get rich [teaching] but one doesn't teach for money, but to help.' (18/AFm) Repeatedly, I heard admonitions against giving into the 'gold chain theory,' the idea that in order to make teaching more attractive to some minorities you must make a display of wealth and status.

Some teachers clearly separated their values from those of the youth of today. I found it interesting that several had difficulty seeing young people subscribing to the same basic values that had motivated them to go into teaching. This inability to see themselves reflected in their students appeared to be one of the main reasons that they could not and did not recommend teaching as a profession. Teaching required sacrifice and caring. Young people, according to some of the teachers, just didn't have what it takes:

> If you look at kids' lifestyle, and ours, it's totally different. Basketball shoes are the main issue. They think if you don't have the same materialistic values, there is something wrong with you or you don't have money.
>
> (92/AFm)

'Kids look for money and prestige. They want something that will set them apart, like clothes, a car.' (90/AFf)

Other teachers framed their arguments in terms of socioeconomic class rather than in opposition to youth in general. The assumption was that low-income kids did not see the benefit of education; they had already given up on a legitimate track out of poverty: 'Low-income kids are not interested in teaching. They are into self, mostly interested in money in the shortest point in time' (41/AFf); 'Money is in the street. That's not what it's about. If they don't value the same things as the dominant culture, they go hustle on the street; they'll get money their own way' (94/AFm); 'If they are in a single, low-income family, they are already dreaming of making a lot of money and hearing from the media that teachers don't make enough money.' (19/AFf) I couldn't help but wonder in listening to the litany of youth lost to material concerns what role teachers themselves played in disseminating misinformation about their own profession. Where are kids getting these views? For working-class kids, their teachers are some of the few college-educated professionals that they actually know personally. Are we inadvertently undercutting the image of our own profession?

Inevitably, in any conversation about money and youth, particularly for young African American males, the model of the successful and wealthy athlete arises. The excessive amount of income that celebrity athletes receive caused concern for many of the teachers. On the one hand, teachers believed that the priorities of our society are misplaced and that teachers should be the recipients of such wealth. As one teacher explained: 'Pay is an issue with teachers because we're taken for granted, no status; athletes get six figures. To shape someone's mind, thought process, is important.' (101/AFm) On the other hand, the high income offered to sports stars undercut teachers' efforts to get kids focused on academics. The chimerical rewards of sports far outweighed anything that they could propose as an alternative. Low-income kids who perceive that they are already behind in the academic world may opt to compete on the football field or basketball court instead. Clearly irritated by the assumption that kids could forego their education for the faint prospects of success in sports, one teacher posed the poignant question: 'Where would athletes be without education?' (67/AFf) Although the answer to this may seem irrelevant to kids still in K-12, it is interesting that most of the African American male teachers interviewed entered college on sports scholarships and went into teaching because they saw it as the only way for them to continue coaching, their first love. Many of these men have gone on to be powerful and effective teachers.

Economic reasons: Too much education for the return

Many of the teachers interviewed had the view that their profession held unrealistic expectations for them in terms of advanced study. Several thought, incorrectly, that teachers are one of the few groups required to continue their education past a terminal degree, and that the number of years that they attend school prior to that degree far exceeds that of other professions that garner higher wages and status. African Americans were particularly upset about the requirement of advanced study for teachers beyond the Bachelor's degree. They argued that most other professions were content with a B.A., whereas teaching required a fifth-year of schooling plus on-going training. They claimed that the extra year prohibits many people of color from entering the field of teaching. Speaking candidly on this issue, one teacher observed: 'Minority people go to college *to get a job*, not to listen to some special lectures or learn for learning's sake. Why should a Black person go to school an extra year to end up with a job that pays less than those that only take four years?' (28/AFf) This apparent discrepancy between more education and lower pay was seen as one of the main reasons that students of color were not entering the field of teaching. As a Black male teacher said:

> In the past because our parents weren't educated, they respected those who were educated. The economic system was more intact, you made more money the more education you had. Nowadays, a mechanic earns more than a teacher, so why should kids want to go to college?
>
> (80/AFm)

As discouraging as these attitudes might be, for many, the reasons for resisting teaching as a prospective profession were far more complex than simply the perceived low salaries. Several informants made this explicitly clear in commenting: 'I don't think it's a pay issue.' (69/AFf) (43/AFf) (18/AFf) One elaborated more fully: 'It would be difficult to attract them (students of color) into teaching even if there was more pay; they still wouldn't come into teaching. I can't convince people to become teachers.

They must have the love of children, then money doesn't matter.' (68/AFf)

Economic reasons: More opportunities elsewhere

If low pay is not the most compelling reason for students of color resisting teaching as a profession, what is? About one-third of the teachers thought that it had to do with the increase in career options available to these students. These perceptions were seldom tempered by economic or social realities or the fact that, because of inequities, many people of color are barred from access to education that would prepare them for professional careers (Wilson, 1991; Sklar, 1995). The range of opinions regarding this view varied greatly, yet most fell into the following three areas: an open marketplace, high aspirations, and historical reality.

The most common perception among the teachers interviewed was that we live in a world today where people can become whatever they want to be. This idea of an 'open marketplace' in which anything was possible, especially for African American males, came most frequently in comments such as the following: 'They could be lawyers or bank presidents, why would they want to be teachers?' (28/AFf) Although this view was most often held by African American females, it was also voiced by other ethnic minority groups. A twenty-five year-old Japanese woman commented: 'A Black male can get paid a lot more in other fields, it's wide open.' (75/ASf) There was little analysis as to who these individuals were or what kind of preparation they had. Somewhere along the line these teachers had bought into the idea that if you are an African American male, you can walk into any job and demand your salary.

The second area of new opportunities could be called 'high aspirations.' Although this is related to the first area, it had less to do with society's views of the individual than with one's upbringing and socialization. A few African American women commented that 'Black men are raised to have high aspirations.' (84/AFf) Another spoke of it in terms of socioeconomic class rather than race: 'If you are a first-generation college student, your parents have such high hopes and expectations. Why would you subject yourself to teaching when there are so many other interesting fields?' (74/AFf) This class analysis was echoed by others who provided a more tempered view on life's options. As one teacher reflected: 'Those who can afford to go to college are from middle-class families and want more options.' (45/AFf)

Several African American male teachers provided a counterpoint to the views of the female teachers mentioned above and gave a significantly different twist to the whole issue of aspirations. They presented a complex set of motivations and circumstances, leaving the reader to mull over the issues of culture, upbringing, parental, and community influences: 'The fear of failure is great for African American youth raised in the inner city' (42/AFm); 'Black males set their visions so high. We project higher than where we feel comfortable rather than take a job within our comfort zone. Then we don't take the jobs in between and end up with lower level jobs that don't provide good self-esteem.' (85/AFm) Another informant drew a rather surprising conclusion based on the reality of residential and educational isolation: 'African Americans may be hesitant to work with other people because of lack of exposure.' (78/AFf)

The third area of increased options focused on the historical reality that many people of color were once barred from most professions. Some of the interviews made it poignantly clear that this was not so very long ago. In fact, at least five of the teachers, who were over sixty years old, remembered when: 'It [teaching] used to be the only thing that Blacks could go into.' (11/AFf) Individuals from groups who have been shut out of certain professions for so long want access not only to the jobs themselves but to the financial rewards that such participation is supposed to bring. Since teaching was a profession in which African Americans had already proven themselves, they wanted to try their hand at areas previously closed to them and/or where they perceived the greatest doubts in White society that they could succeed, such as in the fields of math and science. To understand the scope of the prevailing attitude that students of color are theoretically able to have their pick of professions, I probed further in those interviews where open access was not mentioned. A Black male teacher countered with his reality:

> I don't hear kids talking about wanting to be doctors and lawyers. In the last nine years I have only heard one student say they wanted to be a lawyer and one a doctor. When I sit down to talk to them about college, most don't have a plan. They get discouraged. I ask them, How you going to get to college? Look at your grades? Do you have $10,000?
>
> (92/AFm)

An African American woman echoed that refrain:

> Some kids say that they want to be a lawyer, kids are living in fantasy land; it's what they see on TV. They're not in homes where they have professional families staying up late doing homework. They don't know how much it takes to be a lawyer. Kids only see glamour, nice cars, nice clothes. Even those who are failing think that they are going to college. It's the deception of the media. They don't know what it all entails. Even when they see Black professionals all they see are the clothes. Until they know reality, we can't motivate them. They are out of touch with reality.
>
> (90/AFf)

Educational reasons: Inadequate and negative experience in K-12 schooling

Experience with the educational system is fundamental to understanding why some young people choose to go into teaching and some do not. Although social and economic obstacles can greatly affect which occupations a person selects, usually it is at the classroom level that students see first hand how the teaching profession plays itself out. How students see their teachers, how they are encouraged by the system and the ways in which they are labeled and responded to will mark their lives forever. We must be more cognizant of how 'recruitment' and discouragement toward teaching as a career take place early in their K-12 context.

African Americans were far more reticent than the Latinos or Native Americans to acknowledge the role that poor K-12 schooling played in the decision not to pursue teaching as a career. It was not until some of the teachers saw the connection between lack of adequate preparation for college and the shortage of teachers of color that they began to express their upset with inequities in the educational system. One African American teacher lamented: 'Education has given up on Black children.' (63/AFf) Others concurred: 'We are underhandedly steering children away from education' (71/AFf); 'There are gaps in the education of students of color' (83/AFf); 'The preparation to get into college is overwhelming, especially for minorities.' (94/AFm) One teacher believed that the reason that few minority students select teaching as a career is that, 'They can't keep up; so they do something less difficult than teaching.' (101/AFm)

Almost one-third of all teachers noted negative experiences in school, in contrast to poor academic preparation, as a reason students of color opt not to stay in education for their life work. Two comments see the 'turn off' in terms of timing and are rather gentle in their accusations: 'They just finished high school; they're not thinking about more school' (87/AFm); 'They dread going to college after just coming out of a negative experience.' (61/AFf) Some explained the resistance as a result of boredom. As Goodlad (1984) revealed in his study, *In A Place Called School*, most students are bored by high school, either the curriculum isn't challenging enough or it isn't relevant to their lives. For many, high school is a social wasteland with little academic value. If this is true for the majority of students, how much more true might it be for students of color if they are not incorporated into and engaged with the educational process?

Other teachers expressed their concerns about negative experiences more poignantly. Many of them either had had unpleasant experiences in school themselves or they had watched kids of color over the years pushed aside, misunderstood, or simply lost in the system. Their voices are important to hear: 'Education, as it's set up for minority students, is teaching them to be failures' (16/AFf); 'The forty percent drop-out rate for minorities is due to what happens in the classroom' (33AFf); 'It's not the teaching career specifically. The whole educational environment is very limiting for Black students; there's an element of alienation and culture shock' (16/AFf);

> I think that in education in general, we are failing Black children. In the early stage they are identified as unsuccessful or in need of remediation and are turned off of education as early as the first or second grade. They should not be labeled as unable to succeed.
>
> (17/AFm)

These statements leave us with a greater awareness of the powerful role that teachers play in the career decisions of youth. Without equitable access to a quality education, kids do not even have the choice of going into teaching or not. If they feel disengaged, cheated, or marginalized, they will not know if it is the teacher, the system, or education itself that has turned against them. As one teacher clearly put it, 'If kids are getting turned off of K-12 education, why would they want to teach anyone else?' (71/AFf)

Educational reasons: Lack of support in college

Those students of color who do survive the potentially negative experiences of K 12 schooling and acquire a high school education face still another impediment, success in college. One-fifth of the teachers, reflecting on their own college days, questioned the rhetoric of concern for students of color. One African American woman spoke candidly:

> I live in the [Black] community and I know what it thinks of the [university]. It is viewed as not a positive environment for minorities. The community does not see it as a friendly place. No one [from the university] comes into the schools to promote teaching; no one encourages minorities to apply. There is no program that supports minorities throughout their undergraduate experience. I went to [the university] and I know.
>
> (78/AFf)

Students of color who enter universities and colleges across the United States are faced with multiple challenges. Not the least is an attempt to maintain a sense of self separate from the images and labels that others are ready to place upon you. Children from middle-class families often feel compelled to deny their class privilege and take on the cloak of oppression. They are at times torn between soaring with the freedom and accolades that can come with demonstrating competence within academia and retreating into safe havens where the complexity of one's life is collapsed into a narrow interpretation of one's talents. Universities provide little support for assisting students of color in grounding them in their differences as well as their similarities. Although lack of financial support is most frequently seen as an obstacle for students of color continuing in school, I would advocate that it is in the realm of emotional and intellectual mentoring that students of color are in most need (Gordon, 1997a). This may in fact be a generational issue. Many of the teachers interviewed held the view that college is too expensive for most students of color. Few of them seemed aware of alternative funding. The situation was locked up; the wealthy have access to education, the poor do not.

Social/cultural reasons: Racism

Several of the interviews were filled with accusations of racism – not in a hostile tone, but rather one of resignation and regret. One African American teacher sighed: 'The racial aspect is always there. Why should minorities go back into schools as teachers when there has been so much prejudice for so long.' (76/AFf) Another, disillusioned by the parade of reforms, concurred: 'Racism, it's the old boy policy. People in teacher education don't even seem aware of it.' (10/AFm) Given the ostensible push to recruit more teachers of color and the assumption that school districts need more teachers who can understand the needs of children from all walks of life, more than a few teachers claimed that 'Even if they did get in [to a teaching credentialling program] they couldn't get a job because of color.' (21/AFf) A young African American male's story exemplified this situation:

> I wanted to come home to Cincinnati to teach, but never got a response from the district, so I had to do another job, loading trucks, because I couldn't get hired as a teacher. I subbed for six months but never heard from anyone about my credentials. Finally I got a long-term, two-year, sub position, and [due to circumstances] ended up staying. A mulatto friend of mine with a Master's degree also had to sub. Is it because we're Black that we have to sub?
>
> (44/AFm)

An elderly African American man lamented:

> I kept getting riffed, no seniority, so I got a call to come and teach here [an alternative school for drop-outs]. Strange, the district will go out of state to recruit minority teachers, then riff them in the first year. A lot of minority people who were brought here are not teaching anymore. Uncertainty discourages them. There is a higher pay scale here than in the South but it's a big change to move from the South. The educational philosophy is so different in the South.
>
> (103/AFm)

Social/cultural reasons: Lack of encouragement and racelessness

Lack of encouragement to pursue teaching as a career came on all sides from all groups. Students whose academic performance was less than stellar were seen as incapable of being teachers. Outstanding students were to save their talents for higher paying jobs. Low-income students were presumed to lack the funding for advanced schooling. Middle-class students of color were thought to view the profession as beneath them. Although some of this lack of encouragement might be attributed to parents who may not be aware of or involved in formal schooling, there is significant *discouragement* coming from counselors and middle-class parents who know the benefits of an education. Much of this bias against the field is based on parental and student experiences but it is also an issue of elitism.

In addition to the discouragement that students of color receive from adults at school and in the community, they also have to contend with the norms set by their peer group. For inner-city youth these standards for acceptance can be academically devastating. Fears that demonstrating an interest in school will be equated with 'acting White' and adopting the 'dominant culture's' values impede many urban youth from putting forth their best effort. Such a condition has been called 'racelessness' since it implies that students give up their own racial identity in the process of becoming educated (Fordham and Ogbu, 1986). One African American teacher reflected on the phenomenon: 'I confront students daily who say, "You can't make me learn." It's not cool to be educated. There is a thin wall between success and failure. Blacks can easily turn off from you.' (38/AFf) Although the concept of racelessness is usually associated with African Americans because of Fordham's work with this population, I found this attitude more prevalent with Native Americans as will be seen in Chapter 4.

Do African American Teachers Recommend Teaching?

About seventy-five percent of the African American teachers interviewed did not recommend teaching as a career option to their students or to their friends and relatives; in fact, they discouraged it. Current efforts to recruit African American youth into teaching are stigmatized by the history of segregation. The majority of teachers whom I interviewed held the perception that Blacks who can attend college should venture out into professions previously closed to them. Some do not see this as discouragement but rather as a broadening of horizons: 'I don't specify teaching as a profession; I think they should find their own fulfillment. But I inspire them basically to succeed.' (84/AFf)

Some teachers hesitated when asked about recommending teaching to their students, claiming that it was the rare student who seemed fit for the profession. The standards for future colleagues are revealed in these comments: 'I recommend only to a special type of person, one who has commitment, is open, patient, selfless, and wants to transfer knowledge to others' (37/AFm); 'Yes, oh yes, [I recommend] but they're rare. I encourage the helpful ones, not the honor role students. They have to not take things personally; they have to love kids. You can't teach it but you can make them aware of it.' (61/AFf) Other teachers flatly do not recommend teaching because of their own personal upset with the profession. These teachers put it on the line: 'No, I tell kids there are things more rewarding than teaching. There are so many obstacles to overcome, societal pressures' (55/AFf); 'No, I recommend they get more money, like a computer analyst. I wouldn't tell kids to be a teacher. I only went in because I wanted to be a coach' (42/AFm); 'No, I do not recommend. My kids see how hard I work and they don't want to be like that. My daughter wants to be a writer or a doctor. My son, an architect or involved in sports.' (74/AFf)

A few teachers, very few, were in the vanguard promoting their profession. They revealed how at times they had to go against their spouses, their family and community on a one-person quest to stay the tide of defection from the profession and encourage students of color to take responsibility for the education of the next generation of children. One proud woman told me the story of how her daughter had decided to go into teaching, but not without a great deal of struggle against her father's wishes:

> My daughter is doing her student teaching here at [XXX]. When they were young, my children would come to school with me, helped in my classes, doing bulletin board, etc. My husband tried to steer her away from teaching but she always wanted to be a teacher. She said 'mom, I think you're the best teacher I've known.' None of her [daughter's] friends who are minorities are in teaching; there is a lot of peer pressure to go into something else.
>
> (53/AFf)

One afternoon, after a long interview with an African American male teacher, he concluded our conversation with these powerful words: 'Yes, I recommend teaching. These kids must know that they are needed to educate future generations. I tell them, "if not you, then who?"' (59/AFm) This reminded me of another comment made by a teacher who had done his time in inner city schools both as a student and now as a teacher: 'Young Black males must realize that they are the solution to today's urban problems. Without them we will not survive.' (124/AFm) The desire for expanding horizons of opportunities surely cannot be faulted, but while children are encouraged and pushed to go on to be doctors, lawyers, and engineers, who is opening up the doors to a new generation of teachers of color? Who indeed will teach our children?

3 Latino Teachers

The Construction of a Latino History with American Schooling

The history of the Latino educational experience in the United States, although different from the African American, is one fraught with similar hostility, misunderstanding, and distrust (San Miguel and Valencia, 1998; Moore and Pachon, 1985). Basic to an understanding of educational opportunities for Latinos is the importance placed politically on bilingual education (Fernandez and Guskin, 1981). Although African Americans saw the main battle to be fought on the field of integration with the hope of increased resources, Latinos, particularly Mexican Americans, have sought improved educational access and success through bilingual education. The ironic result has been that, in tandem with residential discrimination, 'bilingual education,' as it has been traditionally administered rather than as it is imagined to operate, has tended to reinforce segregated schooling. Latino students are more segregated today than at any other time in the past (Orfield and Eaton, 1996).

Separation based on language and last name affiliation came in spite of the fact that legislation provided for the integration of public schooling for Mexican Americans about a decade *before* Brown vs. Board of Education began the dismantling of segregated public schools for African American children. In the 1946 Mendez vs Westminister School District case, the court ruled in favor of Mendez stating that separate schools with the same quality of facilities did not mean that they were equal (Gonzales, 1990). Two years later, this was reaffirmed in the Delgado vs. Bastrop Independent School District case. Resistance to segregation in its earliest form, however, came much earlier in the 1930s in a complicated case in Texas between Salvatierra and Independent School District. The court's findings in the case of Hernandez vs. Board of Education in California said that Hispanics were not Black and therefore not subject to the Plessy vs. Ferguson ruling that allowed separate but equal schools for Black children. In 1947, after heated debates, the courts ruled that schools could legally separate Latinos from

Whites. This was partially based on the premise that integration had been accomplished if Latinos and African Americans attended the same schools.

Not until the 1970s did we see court decisions in the Keyes vs. Denver School District case and in Ciscernos vs. Corpus Christi bringing Latinos and Whites together in the same school. Such a move required that Mexican Americans be identified for the first time as a separate ethnic group, not White, for the purposes of public school desegregation (Salinas, 1971). What is interesting about this turn of events was that the point of contention was not that segregation was illegal but that some Mexican Americans did not want to be considered and classified as separate from White Europeans. Looking at census figures dating as far back at 1790, we find that with only one exception in 1930, Mexican has never been viewed as a separate racial category. For the year 2000, a much more amorphous 'Hispanic' category will be added to the census under ethnicity (Fukurai and Davies, 1998).

The Keyes' decision called not only for physical integration but for increased access to education in America through the enhancement of English language learning. As a result, bilingual education became the focal point of Latino political action and resource allocation. The focus on language maintenance inadvertently reinforced segregation. Although segregation in and of itself should not make a difference in one's education, it has proven to do so in United States schools (Valdes, 1998). In many situations in the United States, children in low-income schools that have a predominance of minority youth tend to receive a lower quality of education. This has proven particularly true in poorly run bilingual classes for Latinos if teachers are not fluent in both Spanish and English, if children are misassigned, and if teachers are unqualified to teach rigorous subject matter in a relevant and engaging manner (Auerbach, 1995; Fairclough, 1992).

Public school integration for Latinos raised the familiar question of 'who would teach the children?' As in the African American case, integration came at a price. Desegregated schools meant that the teachers in mixed classrooms would be White (Contreras and Valverde, 1994). Many native Latino teachers who were committed to the education of their people, sharing a common culture and common language, lost their jobs. Latino teachers who had provided leadership and direction in the community found themselves outside the educational system and unemployed (Olneck and Lazerson, 1988).

Although educational aspirations of Latinos remain high, lack of understanding of the American school system combined with minimal schooling, leaves many Latino parents, particularly immigrants from rural Mexico and Central America, ignorant of the negative repercussions of segregated schools (Trueba, 1998; Orfield and Eaton, 1996). In addition to the increasing isolation of Latinos both within schools via bilingual education programs and between schools via residential segregation, some Latino parents question the role of schooling in their families. De La Vega's (1951) conclusions from interviews of more than forty years ago are validated today in the statements given by Mexican Americans in this research that echo the fear that the more schooling that children receive, the less they will identify with their family and culture. In seeing schooling as subtractive rather than additive acculturation (Gibson, 1991b), parents wonder how far the socialization received at school will take them away from their traditional values, customs, and community. This apparent sacrifice is partially because of the fact that schooling continues to demand as part of the price of professionalization the relinquishing of ethnic ties. It is the loss of this connection that paradoxically then leaves the ethnic community on a loose footing, without support or grounding that can be provided by teachers of the community.

Nevertheless, lack of awareness by teachers of the complexity of cultures and values that can be found under the umbrella 'Latino' remains one of the major concerns for parents (De Hoyos, 1961; Valdes, 1998). Assumptions of homogeneity either among all children with a Spanish surname (who may or may not speak Spanish) or all children who speak Spanish is ludicrous and dangerous. The type of cultural capital that highly educated, upper middle-class Mexican or Chilean parents can provide for their children, for example, is radically different from that of an immigrant farm worker's family. Ironically however, time in the country has not proven to be an asset for many Mexican Americans whose academic achievement remains exceedingly low (Rumbaut, 1995). In 1990 less than half of the Mexican American population 25 years and older had completed at least four years of high school (Aguirre and Martinez, 1994). The latest report on high school completion for Hispanics shows a current rate of just over fifty-seven percent (Wilds and Wilson, 1998).

Ways to identify and address the different needs and resources held by students who either self-identify or are labeled as Latino, Mexican American, Latin American, Central American, and/or as one of the many Indian peoples of those regions, etc. may yet be one of our most daunting educational tasks. The dilemma demands immediate attention as Latinos continue to be the fastest growing population in the United States while having the lowest overall academic performance.

The Image of Teaching and Latino Teachers

Latino teachers, especially Mexican Americans, made frequent reference in their interview responses to their 'home country' as a source of educational and occupational values. Many of the informants were in contact with family 'back home' and frequently visited Mexico or had someone visiting them from Mexico. The uniqueness of this situation for Mexican and Central American immigrants as contrasted with other immigrant groups has been discussed by several authors and reminds us of the importance of both proximity to the home country and the role of the extended family in shaping attitudes (Garcia, 1995; Garcia-Castanon, 1994; Suarez-Orozco, 1991). Within Latino culture, as is true within most traditional cultures, respect for education is enhanced by the respect for authority, adults, and teachers. This is then reinforced by a fairly rigid socioeconomic class structure that is often primarily defined by one's educational status (Haycock and Duany, 1991). Education within Latin American countries is seen as a privilege, not a right (Abalos, 1986). With few exceptions, class determines who has access to schooling and to what degree. As a result, education beyond elementary level can appear, on the one hand, prestigious, but, on the other hand, excessive, depending on the socioeconomic priorities in one's life (Valverde, 1987).

Many of the Latino informants were convinced that respect for teachers would increase if teachers themselves honored the culture and traditions of their students. At times this appeared to go against the American concept of compulsory schooling as a right not a privilege. They claimed that if teachers understood that in many Latin countries education is reserved for the elite and that working-class youth are often expected to assist the family financially after a certain age, they would be less inclined to misinterpret students' actions. If students left school early to work (dropped out) or took time off to take care of their family or return home for holidays or celebrations, this should not be seen as disrespectful of teachers but rather respectful of family needs and priorities. When I asked how these attitudes might affect the number of students who are able to select teaching as a career, I was told the following:

> In middle-class Hispanic communities, the image of teachers has changed. But for the lower class, those in this area, it's a week-to-week existence. They are just concerned with getting through the day. They know to send their kids to school, but they are not concerned with what is going on in school. For them, they may not even have a perception of teachers.
>
> (13/LAm)

The issue of class, however, was far more complex than simply assuming that the better educated one's parents, the greater respect one has for teaching. In fact, some teachers claimed that just the opposite was true: 'It depends on who you are talking to – the working class respect teachers more; professionals don't. The issue of respect is complex and intertwined with status.' (8/LAm) Some teachers actually argued that, for Latinos, socioeconomic class was *more* significant than ethnicity, stating that it is the primary determinant in affecting attitudes and actions towards education and occupational aspirations.

The Latino teachers in this study, self-identified as Mexican, Puerto Rican, Cuban, Honduran, or Nicaraguan, believed that teachers continue to receive respect from their students and that teachers, in general, are respected in the Latino community. Their comments contrasted sharply with those of the African American teachers. A Cuban ESL teacher claimed that she had the best and the easiest job in the world largely because she was working with kids who were respectful, motivated, and determined to learn English. Teachers of color from non-Latino ethnic groups, however, did not see Latino students as such a joy to educate. Their perception was that Latino parents did not respect teachers and that Latino youth were disrespectful of teachers. This contrast intrigued me. Were Latino students giving one face to Latino teachers but a radically different one to their 'other' teachers? Were the expectations different from the Latino teachers or were they simply reading the cues differently? Was there any difference between how a Mexican child might respond to a Cuban teacher versus a Mexican American teacher? I did not come up with all the answers but part of the resolution seemed to come down to communication. Latino teachers were able to talk to parents in Spanish; they were sensitive to the class and cultural differences between 'Hispanic' groups; and they were more willing to contact parents personally. Latino students in their classes were apparently less hesitant to speak up and, hence, were more actively engaged in learning, which could explain fewer disciplinary problems. Clearly, these attributes exemplify what Shorris (1992) calls 'cultural translators': 'Hispanics respect teachers. Parents see teachers as one place to go with problems. If they are in trouble, they go to the pastor or to the teacher. They see teachers as leaders. Teachers have a status.' (4/LAm)

The variation in the degree of respect attributed to teachers by the Latino community was greatest, however, between those who had recently come to the United States and those who have been here for several generations. This difference in attitude appeared partially related to class but more so to the assimilation of the 'dominant culture's' values. An African American teacher offered her view on the variations within the Latino community as related to respect: 'First generation are more serious; second [generation], are more acculturated. Adults who need English respect the teacher, those most recently from Mexico. Younger people often don't as much.' (15/AFm) This gradual decline in respect for teachers the longer young people are in America caused major concern for many of the teachers since it often correlated highly with decline in respect for family and elders. Many teachers resented the replacement of traditional values, often conservative and religious, with (north) American materialism and lack of reverence for hierarchy. Two teachers shared their concern about the infiltration of American values:

In my society [Honduras] teaching has a lot of respect. With new immigrants you still have the respect. But those who have been here longer get their values from their peers and it is really bad to be a teacher's pet.

Teachers in the Mexican American community are not respected as much. Here you have to deal with students' disrespectful behavior and the general public's idea that teaching is not a good job.

(9/LAf)

Yes, Hispanic culture does reinforce teaching and education. This is in contrast with the larger culture [American] that stresses money over education. Teaching is valued but students are not encouraged to go into teaching because it is not seen as significant, more like baby-sitting. Personally, I think it is one of the most sane professions there is.

(72/LAm)

From these comments it is clear that, for Latinos, one of the major challenges in the education for Latino youth and eventually their selection of teaching as a career is to gain a greater understanding of the negative influence that urban American working-class culture can have on immigrant values. As emphatically stressed in the interviews, immigrant children and their parents come to this country not only with a strong respect for education, teachers, and the profession, but many actually come *because of* educational opportunities they perceive to be available in the United States that are unavailable in their home country. In the majority of cases individuals are not transferring negative attitudes from their home country to the United States, they are learning these once located in the United States. These findings are consistent with those of other authors who have noted a correlation between the decrease in academic achievement and aspirations with length of residence in the United States (Suarez-Orozco, 1989; Steinberg, 1996; Kao and Tienda, 1995).

Why the Shortage of Latino Students in Teaching

Approximately one-fourth of all the teachers in the present study pointed to lack of academic preparation as a *primary* reason for the shortage of teachers of color. This perception was particularly strong for Latinos and Native Americans who saw the failure of their children in the school system as the main reason for their absence from college campuses and, therefore, from the teaching profession. Even though more students of color are graduating from high school than ever before, this does not necessarily mean that the quality of their education has improved dramatically or that their chances of graduating from college have increased. This is particularly true for low-income youth or those who have attended large urban schools (Wilds and Wilson, 1998).

Inadequate K-12 schooling

According to the informants, the issue of Latino youth not entering teaching as a profession has less to do with resistance to the idea of becoming a teacher because of low status or meager income than it does with lack of success in moving through the academic pipeline. Latino teachers were overwhelmingly preoccupied with the poor academic achievement of Latino students and scoffed at the concern for more Latino teachers. Many of them lamented the low graduation rates from high school and the lack of rigor presented in coursework in many predominantly Latino schools. One teacher made the claim that:

> One out of every three students in the Hispanic community will drop out of high school. Out of two students finishing high school, maybe one will go to college. In many cases this student will not finish college because of the financial pressures of college.
>
> (9/LAf)

Another estimated that 'One out of ten graduate from high school' and concluded by saying: 'Hispanics don't even think of career; they don't make it through high school.' (7/LAf)

Similar frustration arose over testing requirements. Although the comments in this chapter reflect the views of Latino informants, the process of testing for teacher competency was seen by many of the teachers interviewed as one of the most significant factors in limiting minority students' access to the teaching profession. Without sufficient knowledge of English and American culture as used in the examinations, it is difficult to demonstrate one's pedagogical competency. Measuring the qualities of an effective teacher via tests, although fraught with problems, is one of the few ways that parents perceive they can assess whether or not their children are being taught by literate individuals who have a command of basic skills. The complexity of the situation is reflected in this discussion about CBEST (California Basic Education Skills Test):

> I know of a Mexican woman who can't pass CBEST. They won't give her more time. She passed two parts, but can't get the third in reading. There are five teachers here from other states who have come to ... [in California] for a year or two, but who, because they couldn't pass CBEST, changed fields. Hundreds of minorities are interested in teaching but the institution stops them. Luckily, I didn't have to take the test. Do you know of the flaw in the system? If you don't take CBEST, you can teach [on emergency]; but if you take CBEST and fail, you can't teach at all ... I have friends who teach in Catholic schools, but can't pass CBEST. Some have taken the test over and over.
>
> (4/LAm)

'It would be better to put them on probation for seven years, so they can teach and prepare themselves to take CBEST.'

(35/LAf)

Negative experience in school

Only a few of the Latino teachers mentioned negative school experiences as a cause for student resistance to entering teaching. In contrast to this, my later research with Latino college students reflected a much stronger awareness of the many problematic relationships that Latino youth have experienced with the educational system. Their stories relate to misplacement in ESL/LED language classes, inability to use their primary language, ostracization by peers who do not see them as authentically Latino, and frustration with teachers who were unprepared to work with them. These concerns were echoed by only a few of the veteran teachers in this study. Two conversations come to mind but neither held the anger or sense of tragedy expressed in the African American interviews. One Latina recollected her own experience in K-12 schooling. 'I went to a segregated school. All my teachers were Anglo; all students were Latino. We weren't allowed to speak Spanish but we didn't know English very well.' (7/LAf) Another took the idea and extended it to a possible cause for low interest in teaching by Latinos, stating, 'Most high school kids don't see a lot of value in what they just went through. They are reluctant to go into teaching because it is too close to their own experiences.' (13/LAm)

Access to career options

As mentioned earlier, Latino teachers were less concerned about which career their students selected than they were about getting them through high school. The suggestion that perhaps increased access to more job opportunities might be one of the reasons Latino students are not considering teaching as a viable profession left some of the teachers laughing at the thought: 'My students [Latino] don't even think about becoming doctors and lawyers. Teaching would be the last profession that they would choose. They do not see themselves as professionals.' (4/LAf)

Whether this be defeatism or cynicism, the inability to see oneself in the role of an educated person seemed to have developed over years of perceived discrimination. This view highlights the earlier discussion on the influence of American attitudes and values on immigrants. The longer the time spent in this country, the more cynical and resistant the attitudes towards education tend to become. This view is most similar to that expressed by some African American informants who saw the opportunity structure in America as slanted against them, that regardless of degree of effort, doors would still be closed. Here is how one Latino informant saw the situation:

Those who have been here for generations – they are against the system; they have seen that in history being a minority plays a very important role in the jobs you get. They know they won't get the good jobs regardless of education.

(7/LAf)

The few teachers who did see the shortage of students of color in terms of increased options, understood the issue more in terms of supply and demand. From their perspective, since there are 'so few minorities going into higher education, those who are in college tend to go into more lucrative fields.' (13/LAm) Another put it this way: 'Few Hispanics have degrees, those that do, are goal-directed to other careers.' (8/LAm) This view was most often expressed by Latino teachers who saw their role as encouraging the few, often middle-class, students who were clearly academically oriented, to go into high-paying, high-status careers, but rarely into teaching.

Accent discrimination and racism

Discrimination based on accent caused rancor among both Latino and Asian American informants. Some of the Latino teachers who came as immigrants to this country were professionals in their respective fields 'back home.' One teacher who holds several advanced degrees in science was a chemist in Honduras but has not been permitted to teach chemistry in America because of her accent. Instead she is teaching ESL to basic students. She lamented: 'You always have to struggle through the system, then you still have to keep proving yourself even if you make it into teaching. People don't believe you are qualified because of your accent.' (9/LAf) Some teachers claimed that not only had racism tracked them throughout their education, it continues to raise its hoary head even in their professional life. One male teacher explained: 'I persevered, but even now as a teacher I am subject to racism; some people can move beyond it and some can't. This is the basic problem.' (13/LAm)

Lack of encouragement

One of the most important findings in this research noted that teachers from all the ethnic groups agreed that a major reason for the dearth of students of color in the teaching profession is that they are not being encouraged to take academics seriously, and hence, are unable to see teaching as an extension of schooling, as a valuable career choice. The discouragement apparently came from all sides: parents, teachers, counselors, peers, the media, and community people. Most of this, however, was not deliberate. Much was born out of ignorance, lack of information, cultural concerns, and difference in priorities. For many families, the cost of educating a child is great in terms of both human and material sacrifice. Institutions of higher education often require that students leave their family and community to attend college. For some individuals, the cost appeared too high; the move seemed not only unrealistic but perhaps suicidal.

Most of the Latino informants mentioned a need to increase the awareness and knowledge base of parents to enable them to understand better the demands and procedural expectations of schooling and, hence, teaching here in America. The following reflections highlight the need for greater communication and information between school and community: 'Hispanics think that it (teaching) is harder than it is; they're not informed as to what is needed' (31/LAf); 'If they don't know what's available, how can they choose?' (102/LAf); 'A family that is not into education can't imagine education as a job.' (79/LAf)

Beyond the lack of information is the reality that many parents have limited formal schooling themselves. It became clear in the interviews, particularly in Long Beach, that many Mexican American and Southeast Asian immigrant students were sitting in classrooms for the first time in their lives. As these Latino teachers explained: 'Thirty percent of the parents can't read or write; they are from an agricultural community. If there is a discipline problem, parents keep them out of school. Sometimes they are out of school for seven months' (13/LAm); 'There is no compulsory education in Mexico; so some have never gone to school at all' (7/LAf); 'University is for other people. They don't envision themselves as successful in college. Many Hispanics are immigrants; ninety percent are illegal. This leads to "on-again off-again" attendance.' (1/LAm)

The Latino teachers, in particular, spoke of the low expectations that parents had for their children and how this would affect the kinds of jobs for which their children might strive. This did not translate into a lack of caring but rather a difference in degree of emphasis placed on formal education. One teacher explained:

> When kids don't value the score on a test, the teacher and system say, 'See they don't care.' This is the simple solution to the problem. They do care; they just think differently. They don't see the value of education, perhaps because they don't see a lot of people in their environment who have gone through school.
>
> (13/LAm)

From the perspective of these teachers, practical training superseded consideration of a college education in most Latino families. This was usually explained in terms of apprenticing in a trade for men and staying at home to manage a family for women. Although it was clear to me that they were working from assumptions based on their experience with low-income, inner-city students, it was hard to see how these attitudes would have applied to their own children or most middle- and upper-middle-class Latino youth. Seldom, however, did they provide a class-based critique: '[Latino] Parents don't have high expectations of students; they don't feel they have the money to go to college. They think that their kids will get a trade' (4/LAm); 'It is a luxury to think about what you want to do in the future, about going to college. This image comes from their own community; the environment is one of survival' (5/LAf); 'They follow in a pattern of working and school at the same time.' (102/LAf) One teacher went on to explain in detail how values grounded in traditions, culture, and pragmatism can at times thwart the educational mission:

> [Latino] Parents have a different view of education. It's not the same as Asian or Anglo. Education is important, but it isn't the most important thing. Parents are dealing with survival, not long-range goals. They keep the kids home to do housework, or if another member of the family has a doctor's appointment. Sometimes kids help parents by working after school, some till two o'clock in the morning. They are too tired to learn; they soon realize they can make pretty good money without school.
>
> (7/LAf)

Latinos, as well as many other traditional ethnic minority groups, place a high value on family, helping, and nurturing. The reality of leaving the family and community for college is not seen as beneficial, particularly if it does not in some way provide a return to the community. Although these are honorable values in themselves, some teachers saw them as stifling, especially as they pertained to Latinas. One woman illuminated the situation:

> [Latino] Men often don't want women to get educated because they will know too much. They fear that they [women] will start acting like Americans. We need to re-educate Mexicans in America to accept that girls should go to school. Otherwise girls will be victims of the system, as well as their husbands and family if we don't liberate them. Girls think that they will be taken care of.
>
> (7/LAf)

This was spoken by a migrant woman who married at sixteen years of age without completing high school. After raising her four children, she decided to return to school without her husband's knowledge. Four years later, when she received her AA diploma in the mail, her husband found out and threatened her with a divorce. She has been single ever since and now has a Master's degree.

Low pay

Latino teachers did not see money as a consideration in attracting Latino youth into the teaching profession. Most of them believed that they were well paid and that the benefits that came with the job in terms of security, time off, ease of work load, etc. were bountiful. When I asked one Latina about the frequently heard complaint that teaching is a twenty-four hour a day, twelve-month a year, low-paying job, she smiled at me, incongruously stating:

> As a bilingual teacher I also have aides, so I don't take work home. I'm home by four o'clock. Holidays and benefits are great. Bilingual teachers have the best students. They are highly motivated, attentive and very concerned about getting extra credit. Their homework is always turned in. I get over $50,000 a year for nine months' work. That's more than my husband gets who is an engineer and has to bring work home with him almost every night.
>
> (35/LAf)

Although Lortie (1975) speaks of teaching as being a 'front-loaded career,' these teachers did not see it that way. In fact, many argued just the opposite, seeing the 'first eight years as pretty tough' financially but then things smooth out, raises are automatic and the time you spend in preparation decreases. This was a sore point particularly for those who had worked in other jobs prior to teaching and were entering later in life but were being forced to begin at the bottom of the scale. It was more frustrating still for those who were teachers in other states or who had taught in private schools but were not credentialed. Many complained of not receiving 'seniority credit' for previous work. Some were required to take teacher education courses for up to three years before being credentialed in a state after having already taught for ten years.

On the other hand, those who were credentialed and had stayed in the profession for ten or more years seemed to be doing quite well. An enthusiastic Latino cheered the profession: 'It's a great job once you get established. You move up rapidly on the pay scale. Benefits are great, retirement, contract, credit, stability.' (82/LAm) Others agreed: 'I didn't do it for the money. I get $50,000, for nine months' work with a Master's degree and fifteen years. In 1973 I began at $15,000. Now that's a jump. What other job could provide this?' (35/LAf); 'Money is not the issue. We get $22 an hour as sub, $150 a day; I get $35 an hour.' (35/LAf) It seemed that teachers who had professional family members or friends were able to weigh the benefits of teaching against the salary and had greater respect for the profession, as did this young woman: 'Entry-level attorneys' income are the same as teachers'. I know, my cousin is one (a lawyer) in Connecticut. Even if (teachers) made a lot of money, it wouldn't make a difference; so money is not the real issue.' (79/LAf) Others agreed in a variety of ways: 'We might be underpaid in relation to engineering but we shouldn't be compared to it' (82/LAm); 'Money is not the main thing. Quality of life is important, earth and nature, peace with oneself. The vacations and hours, the creativity in teaching must be considered.' (5/LAf) Or as one Latino teacher pragmatically claimed:

> No one goes into teaching for the money. You cannot make the same money for the same years of education, even though you work only nine months. You have to go into teaching for the love of the work, the kids, the subject matter, or for me, it was coaching.
>
> (8/LAm)

One of the few Latinos who did mention income as an issue muted his concern by saying: 'Even though many Hispanics want to help our people, there's the feeling that I want to make money *and* I want to do those other wonderful things.' (13/LAm)

Concluding Remarks

In comparison to most of the African American teachers interviewed, most of those teachers who self-identified as Latino did not see their job as low status with low pay. I was amazed to see the pride in the profession and the numerous stories that reflected gratitude for a job with good income, security, benefits, and an opportunity to help others. The difference might be explained in several ways. Many of the Latino teachers were bilingual teachers or special education teachers. They worked mostly with immigrant children. If we accept the view of Ogbu, Suarez-Orozco, Rumbaut and others, one could argue that these teachers were working with children who were still traditionally motivated towards education and, therefore, respectful of teachers. Similarly, many of the children's parents were not well educated and unfamiliar with the American system. This provides teachers with authority and power that tends to decrease as their constituents gain advocates within their own families.

The other reason for the difference between the attitudes of African Americans and Latinos might be that many of the Latino teachers are immigrants themselves. They hold some of the same hopes and dreams as their students do. They perceive themselves in professional roles. Some of them have moved from modest means into the middle class. Some of the women have had to give up a great deal, including husbands and families, to continue their education. They are proud of their accomplishments. African Americans, on the other hand, have a powerful historical consciousness about segregated schools in the United States. Some of the informants came from families with two or more generations of highly educated Black professionals. They are not immigrants; indeed, they have seen their progress in education thwarted throughout the more than 300 years of African American history. Their hopes have turned to cynicism. The legacy of great Black teachers is clearly documented as is the fallout from desegregation. Their desire for status and the acknowledgement of their talent is great.

4   Native American Teachers

Native Americans and Their Struggle to Survive Schools

Unwilling to allow Native Americans to provide an education compatible with the needs of their own people, and fearing what they misunderstood, White Americans in the late nineteenth and early twentieth centuries required that Indian children attend boarding schools in which traditional values and native languages were outlawed (Adams, 1988; Kramer, 1991; Lomawaima, 1993). Historically, federal policy towards Indian education has been directed at 'civilizing,' assimilating, and converting Native Americans into the mainstream of American, Christian culture (De Vos, 1980). As a result, Native people came to see government schooling as an attempt to destroy their culture, their way of thinking, and any links to their children (Unger, 1977).

Native Americans have a long tradition of educating their own children whereby many 'teachers' participate in the training (Marashio, 1982). Elders serve as guides for the younger members of the tribe. Children watch, listen, and follow long before they act. Each member of the tribe is perceived as having a useful function and a reason for being (Wilson, 1996). The tribe's survival as well as the life of the individual are based on the ability of the child to comprehend and apply what he/she learns. Within the context of government boarding schools this integration with everyday life was lost. When available, public schooling in any form did not acknowledge the Indian view of education as a means to communicate knowledge accumulated through the ages from one generation to the next (Nabokov, 1991). Native people saw government education as an attempt to convey the knowledge and authority of the dominant culture, usually by members of that culture, to Indian youth. Kluckhohn (1962) lamented the loss of this integration in commenting that Navajo culture had become an ugly patchwork of meaningless and unrelated pieces, whereas it was once a finely patterned mosaic. Many non-Native peoples, however, retain a romantic notion of Native culture, seeing it as both monolithic and tied to spiritual values. The trauma of eradication and negation of first peoples is taken as historical. Few are aware of how the past continues to play itself out in present-day classrooms across the United States (Harmon, 1990). Native children have some of the lowest achievement rates of any ethnic minority group in America (Swisher and Hoisch, 1992). Studies from the Meriam Report demonstrate that not only do the majority of Indian children achieve poorly in schools but they do not learn skills that lead to employment after graduation (Kluckhohn, 1962).

Ironically, for many Native peoples it is not even a question of choosing between acquiring the skills, knowledge, and lifestyle of mainstream middle-class society or retaining one's cultural identity and traditions. Seldom is either avenue being offered. Deyhle (1992) argues that compulsory education has, in fact, been a major factor in removing Indians from their tight-knit tribal world and throwing them into an intensely individualistic one without the necessary cultural defenses to survive psychologically. A Native teacher called this process 'cultural dissonance with the White man's ways; the ability to read but not decode.' (36/NAm) On reservations across the United States, Native peoples struggle to understand how they can gain self-sufficiency, free of dependence on the 'outside' world of federal agencies, which are often flawed with bureaucratic and political agendas, a dependence paradoxically created as a legacy from federally provided government schooling guaranteed by treaty. Can an urban education equip Indian youth for leadership back on the reservation? Does it even serve as a credible vehicle to bridge the gaps between Indian and non-Indian ways of thinking?

As seen in the following comments gathered in a variety of settings along the west coast of the United States, Native teachers continue to struggle daily with these issues in their attempt to balance the acquisition of skills for success within many different cultures. How a middle-class Indian teacher does this varies greatly depending on their own position both within their tribe and within the educational hierarchy in mainstream society. The interviews in this study both confirm and illuminate the confusion and contradictions American Indians face when confronted with decisions about schooling in the still evident historical legacy of conquest and attempted genocide.

Native Americans: The Image of Teaching and Respect for the Profession

Part of the difficulty in establishing a positive image of teaching or imagining oneself in the profession of educating others is that much of what is taught can seem irrelevant to the needs of traditional and/or working-class families (Stiegelbauer, 1992). In the view of Native American teachers in this study, it was the older members of the tribe who saw little connection between the time spent in school and the functioning of the family or tribal unit. The inability to see the relevance of public schooling to the demands of people's everyday lives plagues many aspiring working-class students, regardless of ethnic heritage, if their parents are not formally educated. It is probably the single most significant factor in prohibiting many adults from supporting the educational efforts of their children and encouraging them to go into teaching. If this perception of ignorance is internalized by parents, they may remove themselves from the educational arena altogether, fearing that they will contribute to the child's failure by not meeting the expectations of the public school teacher. For Native Americans, this absence of parental involvement was palpable. A young Native teacher, thinking back on her own family's image of formal schooling, related: 'Yes, it [education] is respected, but my mom would say "I can't help you, I'm too stupid." She was in awe of it [schooling], but it was nothing that she could identify with; and this began as early as the first grade.' (112/NAf)

For Native people, negative images of schooling have been passed down for generations. Even though students themselves may not have gone through boarding schools, young people have heard the stories and internalized the messages. As one Native teacher explained: 'It [boarding school] was like a prison to them; it's hard to change that mentality.' (109/NAf) Another who worked with 'at-risk' Native youth commented: 'Boarding school told them that they were nothing, so education was not a positive experience.' (111/NAf) The Native teacher who attributed the low academic success of Native youth to 'cultural dissonance' went on to say: 'Education is the equivalent to going to learn how to be a White man.' (36/NAm) This cultural dissonance can result in alienation and a sense of betrayal of class and culture for ethnic minority individuals. Native teachers spoke extensively of their being ostracized from their tribes through the push and pull of reservation life: 'I put on a White face for the day in school, then at home I'd become Indian again. It was exhausting to have to wear two faces. Boarding school fosters this mentality. My mom wanted me to be less Indian.' (110/NAm)

As seen in this interview, the teacher is torn in a variety of ways, not just with the traditional conflict between school and home. Her mother, perceiving that her daughter would be more successful if she stayed within the expectations of school, discouraged her transition back into Indian ways. Clearly, the double consciousness or dual frame of reference (Gibson, 1988) required to survive in both worlds can leave a child torn and frustrated. Asking one young teacher about her family's attitude towards education, I was told:

> Yes, my grandmother was very proud [of my educational accomplishments]. There is an old Indian saying, 'Go my son, go get an education; go my son, get off the reservation.' But I lost my place with my family. My people think I think that I'm better than them, so they resent me [because I am educated].
>
> (77/NAf)

The multiple masks required for success within apparently discrepant contexts can lead not only to confusion of personal identities but resistance to education in general and to teaching in particular. A negative image of teaching and teachers hinders student willingness to stay within the educational process long enough to consider teaching as an option. If schooling is seen as a profession that contributes to the division and disruption of family and community life, why would one select it? A young Native teacher put it this way:

> When I go back to the reservation, people don't know what to say to me; they think I've changed; people don't know how to treat me. It's hard to go home, but that's my safety net when things get bad here [in the city]. Many Indians go back to the reservation after one year away. My family tease me about being an urban Indian; I have to win approval again and again, every time. I'm a different person when I'm there.
>
> (112/NAf)

Some informants believed that the image of schooling and teachers would be more highly respected if the rhythm and demands of traditional Native American life were better understood and honored. Much of the conflict between non-Native teachers and Native students arises over attendance problems during seasonal festivals, naming ceremonies, Pow Wows, initiation rites, funerals, and other cultural events. Participation in such traditional Native gatherings is not only important but necessary for children to learn the knowledge and skills essential to their own heritage and survival. To many middle-class teachers unfamiliar with Native ways, 'skipping school' for community activities is seen as a lack of respect for education. Ironically, these gatherings are what many Native people see as the essence of Native education (Reyhner, 1992). Some teachers believed that the situation could be remedied if there were more Native teachers: 'Yes, education is respected, but teachers are all Anglos so you are not associated with your own.' (30/NAf) As you will read in Chapter Six, replacing White teachers with Native teachers has its own layers of complications.

Native Americans Address the Low Participation of Indian Students in Teaching

Native American informants were more cautious in identifying the reasons for low participation of their people in the field of teaching. For many Native youth, the prospects of continuing on to college in order to acquire a teaching credential were thwarted not only by their family's traditional views but more significantly by poor academic preparation and, hence, low graduation rates from high school and college (Wilds and Wilson, 1998). Racism, lack of teacher and counselor preparation to deal with the complexity of tribal cultures, alcoholism, foster parenting, and confusion over the Native role in contemporary America come together to help us understand both why there is such a need for Native teachers and why there are so few (Reyhner, 1992).

Low high school graduation rates

The primary concern for Native American teachers had little to do with the professional career decision-making process of their students and everything to do with survival through high school graduation. If they could keep students in school, even if they were not academically challenged, they would have succeeded in ways that could perhaps break the cycle of attrition. Native teachers were well aware of the problems that Indian kids face in mainstream public schools. They knew that education in and of itself has been as much the problem as it has been, or ever could be, the solution. Ambiguous educational support from family, community, and friends, combined with latent or worse racism, forces Native kids to search for ways to maintain their own sense of dignity. For some, the most logical choice is to remove themselves from the system. As noted by one of the teachers: 'Indians have one of the highest drop-out rates; they can't get into college. They have the lowest graduation rate; only two percent go on to college.' (36/NAm) For others, hiding their identity tempers the indignities and buffers the insults: 'I was told don't tell anyone that you're Indian. Students want to wash off their culture.' (108/NAf)

Although education on the reservation can be difficult, moving from it can be suicidal. The contrast between reservation life and city life is stark. For many Native people, the movement to a large, anonymous city after years under the watchful eye of family and elders proved daunting. As one Native teacher confided in me: 'I went from being in a school with seventy-five kids on the reservation to a huge urban high school. We usually drop out in the first year.' (110/NAm) Some Native teachers believed that the lack of parental support for education was due to the parents' own failure in the system as well as their lack of understanding of compulsory education. 'There is a lack of familiarity with the advantages of teaching, with what you can do with it.' (12/NAf) But according to most of the teachers, Indian students never even consider teaching as a career and neither do their counselors. Those who are seen as academically solid are tracked into either drafting or business.

Racism

Negative school experiences were most often seen in terms of racial identity. Native American teachers spoke passionately about racism as a cause of their children being dismissed and mislabeled. Stereotypes within the non-Indian culture thwarted the academic effort of these Indian youth: 'My granddaughter was doing great until she told them that she was an Indian, then they treated her differently and her grades dropped, then she had problems.' (113/NAf)

> People thought that my daughter and I were Asian. They don't know about differences. When my daughter told her school friends that she was Native American, they stopped asking her for help. Before, they thought that she was smart [when viewed as an Asian], but not anymore.
>
> (108/NAf)

Another Native American mother, now a paraprofessional in an ethno-centric Indian school, echoed these views:

> I was told by the principal [in a traditional public school] that my daughter couldn't succeed. Stereotypes limit what kids can do. Most students of color don't like school well enough, so they don't want to be a part of the system. My son wanted to start his own school so he wouldn't have to put up with the stereotypes.
>
> (111/NAf)

But the stereotypes work in multiple ways. The assumptions that Indian kids can't succeed are compounded with the community attitudes that if you do succeed you have sold out. A teacher confided in me her sadness and dismay: 'I have one student who told me that he didn't want to be seen carrying books home, so he keeps one there [at home] and one in class.' (113/NAf)

Personal and financial costs of education

As seen in the previous section, the image of teaching has suffered from its historical ties to boarding schools and the erasure of cultural memory. Some Native teachers claimed that their decision to continue their education had cost them dearly. For many, the potential price of ostracization for choosing teaching as a career was too high. They feared not only loss of contact with their culture but also with their family and friends. It is complex. As one Native teacher said: 'Our emphasis is on living with the world; our tradition does not place a value on formal education.' (36/NAm) Concern with the potential cost of higher education and the awareness that government assistance has dwindled over the years led many of the informants to question me as to why a Native student should take the financial risk of attempting the turbulent waters of higher education. As these teachers reminded me: 'Funding for college now is not like it was in the 70s; students don't see a way that they can afford it.' (111/NAf) 'Money isn't there for help like it once was. Education money used to be pumped into the Indian community.' (115/NAm)

No jobs at the end

For those who did take on the challenge and persevere through the academic demands and hoops in an attempt to craft an educational life for themselves, the going did indeed prove to be rough. One Native teacher admitted: 'I'm a product of the boarding school system. It took me longer to get my certificate [ten years] because boarding school didn't prepare me very well for college.' (109/NAm) Another spoke of waiting for two years after she received her credential to teach. She said: 'I wanted to teach in Seattle with students of color, but they never called me.' (77/NAf) She finally went to rural Yakima and found work. Both of these teachers saw the situation as ironic given the lip service paid to increasing minority teachers and the many sacrifices they had to make in order to gain entry into the profession.

Concluding Remarks

As seen from the interviews with Native American teachers, the tension and confusion related to the prospects of Indian youth entering teaching is directly related to the community stories and history based on abuse by government schools and, in particular, boarding schools. The perception lingers that teachers are less concerned with acknowledging and honoring traditional Indian values than they are with eradicating these traditions. Many parents are torn between encouraging their children to stay in school and succeed academically, thus risking the possibility of dilution of family ties, and encouraging them to remain committed to the old ways and resist assimilation. Although there perhaps should not be a contradiction, schooling, as currently defined, has not been amenable to embracing this complexity.

Some parents, however, as reflected in a few of the interviews, try to support their children's academic success by discouraging their identification with traditional ways. Whether this is an attempt to alleviate the burden of a bifurcated existence or to help insure a child's access to the perceived benefits of a positive educational experience, it is difficult to tell from the conversations. What was clear is that the value of schooling in the Native American mind is fraught with contradictions and complexity. If the image of formal schooling is perceived as relating to assimilation into the dominant culture, then the image of those who guide the educational process can be viewed as perpetrators of the dissolution of Indian culture. Young people who have been socialized to see schooling as something that was done to their people to eradicate their 'Indianness,' their relation to family, tribe, and their very existence, are not likely to embrace teaching as a profession. Although this complexity is played out across all four ethnicities featured in this book, it is most vivid in the Native American interviews.

5 Asian American Teachers

Immigration and a New History for Asian Americans

As one of the fastest growing immigrant populations in America, Asian Americans provide a unique challenge to our understanding of diversity. As a result of the Immigration Act of 1964 and the elimination of the national origins quota, large numbers of Koreans and Japanese were allowed to enter the United States. Ten years later with the ending of the Vietnam War, America, in response to the devastation of Vietnamese and Cambodian society, began to admit large numbers of Southeast Asian refugees. Between 1975 and 1995 one million refugees had arrived in America, some of them children without parents (Rong and Preissle, 1997). And in ever increasing numbers, Chinese immigrants from Hong Kong and mainland China have joined longstanding Chinese communities in American cities.

The influx of Asian immigrants since 1965 has led many urban schools to reconsider stereotypes not only of the so-called 'model minority' Asian American but also of who in fact makes up the socially constructed and ill-conceived term 'Asian' (Hartman and Askounia, 1989; Nakanishi and Nishida, 1995). Although we have gradually, but with some difficulty, been able to admit Southeast Asians into the paradigm, we are far less willing to concede or understand the presence of Central Asian and South Asian peoples (Trueba, et al., 1993). The ethnic diversity within the Asian category of United States racial discourse is compounded by major differences in language, religion, politics, and social history (J. Lee, 1991). As the children of these families enter our schools, we are challenged to understand these differences. Yet, this resurgence of Asian immigrant children in urban class-rooms has provoked minimal inquiry into the reasons why there are so few Asian American teachers to assist these children, as well as why there is so little advocacy on the part of parents to have Asian American teachers teach their children. Part of the answer may lie in the discrepancy between American views and Asian views on education and the role of teachers.

At the risk of overly general views, one might characterize American public schooling as part of a social service mission that enlists the largely female teaching force in the task of socializing and civilizing immigrants and workers into an acceptably middle-class consensus of values and literacy (Clifford, 1989). East and North Asian education as exemplified by Chinese tradition, in contrast, brings schooling to the local community with pre-existing hierarchies largely maintained by male teachers whose status rests on the maintenance of strict intellectual standards by which the elite justify their authority (Domino and Hannah, 1987). In this portrayal, the Chinese school-master is first of all an expert, a scholar who deigns to tolerate the local children while screening the few capable entrants for further schooling. American teachers, mostly female, meanwhile build their status on providing basic schooling for all the children of the community (Strober and Tyack, 1980). The stern task of screening in American schools is assigned to testing experts and the demands of scholarship are reserved for the (more likely) male practitioners at the secondary level (Rury, 1989). The task of social discipline is still of primary importance in the American classroom. This is not to say that the Asian model of schooling ignores moral education, far from it, but rather that it is oriented towards the acquisition of knowledge for demonstration in examinations, which, if successful, will take the student out of the community. American education, in contrast, has tended to remain community-based, advocating the development of the 'whole' child as seen in terms of increased independence and self-awareness (Rohlen, 1983).

The Chinese teacher has prestige based on continuing hierarchies that preserve the local culture and its traditional community; the American counterpart finds her mission in the difficult task of social discipline of the newcomers with her scholarly skills consigned to the background (Herbst, 1989b). Facing such a situation, the young Asian Americans who would be teachers experience the confusion of moving successfully toward the role of expert while alienated from the role of teacher by the discrepancies between their varied cultures, both in how schooling is valued and in the respect given to teachers. As students in the United States, Asian Americans gain from the educational mission of American schools both to welcome diversity and reward achievement. As potential teachers, they fear that the combination of disrespect for teachers and a daunting variety of students renders their academic expertise inadequate for the role of teacher as under-stood in Chinese tradition.

The Image of Teaching and Asian American Teachers

The Asian American viewpoint, and this is defined here by interviews with teachers of Japanese, Korean, Chinese, Pilipino and Vietnamese back-grounds, was frequently explained in terms of cultural background. Traditionally, the status of teachers in East Asia has been very high (Baruth and Manning, 1992; S. J. Lee, 1994; Y. Lee, 1991). Based primarily on Confucian values that dictate respect for relationships and hierarchy, Asian cultures have placed teachers in the educated, if not ruling, elite (Smith,

1994). Although this is gradually being eroded by materialist influences that tie status to accumulated wealth (Goodman, 1990), the teachers interviewed had been raised under the more traditional system.

Status in most Asian countries is a product of a tightly woven community in which individuals take responsibility for each other. Teachers were, and still are, seen as conduits to a life beyond the community (Yao, 1988). Social mobility comes through a rigorous meritocratic and competitive testing system where only a few succeed. Teachers who facilitate this success are highly regarded. Closely allied with the Asian concept of teacher is the assumption of respect from students and the community. In traditional Asian culture, the teacher is a model of perfection who is granted prestige based on knowledge and status within the Confucian social hierarchy. Prestige provides income through a range of perks within a closely knit community where status is dependent on the quality of education a child receives and, hence, on the teacher who is responsible for that education (Su, et al., 1997).

Respect based on the Asian model is associated with structure, order, discipline, and reverence, all of which are dubious expectations for Asian Americans considering a career in teaching in American public schools. The likelihood of entering a situation where respect is not conferred based on position but rather on performance frightened many of the teachers as well as students considering a teaching career. They argued that respect for elders, and thus for teachers, is an inherent Asian characteristic: 'respect for elders has nothing to do with fear or authoritarianism; it is just natural for Asians to be respectful.' (181/ASm)

To comprehend further Asian respect for teaching, a Japanese American teacher wanted to distinguish between her people's view of education and other ethnic groups. Her critique was not only intercultural but intracultural, illuminating the differences in attitudes about education *among* various 'Asian' groups:

> Asians have high respect for education, especially Japanese Americans. Their demands for respect are different from other minorities. We are taught perseverance. All our myths, stories, even TV programs are around those who overcame great odds to get where they are. The new wave of Southeast Asians are different; they are from an agricultural background. Many of their parents have never been in a formal school setting before. The earlier immigrants were more highly educated and valued education more. Vietnamese are highly educated, but Cambodian and Laotian are not so.
>
> (75/ASf)

This comparison is significant because most non-Asian Americans associate the socially constructed racial category of 'Asian' as Japanese, Chinese and

Korean, assuming that other 'Asian' groups follow the pattern set out by these more dominant societies. In fact, as this teacher pointed out, most East Asian students who come to the United States are from urban areas where a high degree of emphasis is placed on formal schooling. Southeast Asian students, in contrast, tend to be from more rural communities where education has been deterred because of war and dislocation. Nevertheless, even in these societies teachers have traditionally been held in high esteem. A comment heard in all of the Vietnamese American interviews revealed: 'Vietnamese [teachers] back home are very respected, but not here.' (32/ASf, 89/ASm)

Adapting to the immigrants' new environment has often meant adopting the attitudes and values of mainstream society. As difficult as it might be for many Americans to realize, the lack of respect for education and teaching as a profession is an American phenomenon (Solomon, 1992). As noted previously in reference to other ethnic minority groups and reiterated here once again, it appears that the greater the contact with 'the dominant society,' the less the respect for authority and, hence, for teachers. The words of a young Chinese American teacher illuminate this phenomenon: 'The status [of teachers here] is not as high as in Asian countries. Education is valued [by Asians] but as Asians stay here longer, they become more like Americans and lose respect.' (23/ASf) Another Asian informant wanted to clarify the evolution in attitudes and the distinction between Asian and Asian American value structures: 'In the Asian *American* community, teachers are not seen as prestigious. Asian parents want status for kids. Asians now say that teaching is not good enough.' (97/ASf)

Asian parents, desiring that their children succeed in the 'New World,' try to accommodate to the shift in values. Wanting status and respect in their new country, they buy into the new credo; as one teacher put it: 'In America money equals prestige.' (97/ASf) For some parents it has been difficult to watch their children acquire the ostentatious trappings of wealth at the expense of family values, including respect for elders. For others, however, once they make the association between status and wealth, they steer their children away from helping professions into more lucrative careers. When maintaining 'face' is all important, it is essential that the avenues for status and respect are clearly understood.

Asian American Resistance to Teaching as a Career

As of 1994, Asian American teachers constituted less than two percent of all K-12 teachers with a mean of only eight Asian Americans each enrolled in pre-service teacher education programs in the United States (AACTE, 1994). Low involvement in teacher preparation is not because of any lack of success in education generally. Asian American graduation rates from college increased twenty-two percent between 1989 and 1991 with students moving into professional and graduate schools at least as demanding as teacher education (AACTE, 1994). Given that Asian Americans, in the aggregate, enjoy relatively high academic success through to the level of graduate study, reasons for their lack of involvement in teacher education must be found that vary from the reasons for other minority groups whose low college attendance and graduation levels provide the most obvious explanation for lack of participation in the teaching profession.

Lack of encouragement from parents and community

Negative attitudes toward the teaching profession as held by parents was the number one factor given for Asian American students not choosing teaching. This was particularly true for first- and second- generation students but was also found in third- and fourth-generation informants as well. As one young Asian male said: 'What people want comes from their parents.' (177/ASm) This was not simply a matter of taking another's views into consideration, but rather an almost absolute acceptance of the career expectations, spoken and unspoken, laid out by parents, family and community as related by these two informants: 'Parents don't encourage kids to go into teaching. Even if they're not middle class, parents will encourage their children to be doctors and lawyers' (23/ASf); 'I know that it is a stereotype, but you are pushed in the direction of professions of high status and money, like medicine, law, biz. Teachers don't have the title of Doctor.' (191/ASm)

Prestige and income and stability

Prestige was intricately entwined with high income. The informants moved easily between these concepts as if they were synonymous, noting repeatedly that both are very important within Asian culture. More than half of the Asian American informants directly mentioned parental pressure to enter jobs that enhanced the image of the family. As these informants make clear: 'Asians want prestige for their kids' (176/ASm); 'In Asia, status is gained through a combination of money and power but in the US only money and a fancy car give you status.' (32/ASf) The repeated allusion in the interviews to Asian culture as materialistic grates against the Western image of Asia as a spiritual space at one with nature. Nonetheless, comments such as the following peppered the conversations: 'Asians focus on money; it's a cultural thing' (189/ASf); 'The money issue is an Asian mentality. Maybe after a few generations, that will change.' (178/ASm) Many of the informants not only believed that teachers are not well paid but they actually equated teachers' income with poverty. 'Money is important; if you don't have money, you will go hungry' (166/Asm) followed as a reason for not allowing their children even to consider teaching as a career. Even when countered with the reality that most teachers live a middle-class lifestyle and earn about the same as, or more than, university faculty members, the informants were unconvinced: 'The more you get paid, the better you are treated. University teachers probably get treated like gods.' (154/ASf)

Money was directly related to stability. Although parents claimed that they wanted their children to have financial security, few informants knew that teachers are provided with greater security of employment than almost any other profession. This security is not limited to job tenure, which is usually guaranteed after three years, but takes some less obvious forms such as medical and pension benefits of which the general public seem unaware. Rather, Asian Americans saw teaching as a precarious profession verging on an itinerant lifestyle for those involved. Regardless of the level of awareness on the part of the informants, it is their perception of the profession that is guiding career choices for young Asian Americans. This perception was particularly acute for first-generation immigrants who are looking for stability in their lives and fear being left to struggle as they may have had to back home (Ogbu and Simons, 1998).

Fear of working outside one's comfort zone

External factors such as low pay, low status, and negative image paled, however, against the fear of incompetence in attempting to educate 'someone else's child.' Although this could be simplistically labeled 'racist' or 'isolationist,' we found that many of the informants truly believed that they were unequipped to teach children whose cultural backgrounds differed from their own. Whether this assumption is valid or not, what is important is the *perception* by Asian Americans that they live by a different set of cultural norms, norms that regulate attitudes towards education, status, associates, and careers. Recurring reservations included having to work with disrespectful students, prejudice based on language and accent, reticence towards speaking in public or in front of large groups, and the primacy of maintaining a private life.

The claim made by a variety of informants and echoed in the comment, 'If I have to work with different students, I won't know their thoughts' (169/ASm) had more to do with a sense of cultural integrity than anything else. Non-Asians would neither understand, nor accept, the constraints that Asians place on themselves. This included the degree of respect accorded to elders, the focus on self-control, and the willingness to accept delayed gratification. The flip side of this claim led to the assumption that Asian American teachers would not be able to understand non-Asian students' backgrounds and therefore not be able to teach them in a way compatible with 'their culture.' This awareness led one woman to comment in frustration: 'In China everyone is Chinese so it is easier to communicate.' (164/ASf)

Informants candidly recognized their limited exposure to, and involvement with, other ethnic groups, which they usually defined as African Americans and Latinos, explaining: 'We live in very tight-knit communities; we are very sheltered.' (181/ASm) Because of this isolation, many of the informants believed that they would enter the classroom with a high degree of fear and prejudice. When pressed as to how they thought other teachers currently teach children from a range of backgrounds, one hedged and commented: 'Well, maybe I could teach immigrants.' (177/ASf) The common reasoning was that most immigrants from traditional societies hold similar values in terms of respect for elders and education.

Lack of respect for teachers in the US

Related to the hesitancy to work with diversity were concerns about the ability to control and discipline student behavior. Most of the informants believed that 'students in the United States cause trouble; you can't control them; you won't get respect.' (173/ASm) Many teachers were amazed at the disrespect shown to American teachers by students. In sharp contrast to Asian schools where teachers are revered and in control, teachers in this country seemed at a loss as to how to command respect. As one young Vietnamese woman said: 'I can only speak for Vietnamese people. Teaching is not worth the trouble.' (6/ASf)

Inability to communicate with 'others' and constraints on behavior

Students were described as unruly, undisciplined and gang-oriented. This perceived aggressiveness fed the informants' 'fear of offending people or saying the wrong thing.' (165/ASf) The fear, in turn, extended to students' parents with whom most of the informants believed they would have difficulty relating unless they could draw on an underlying moral authority like that which exists within many Asian American communities. They believed that if a teacher knew the culture and customs of students, the teacher could control most of their behavior by making them accountable to the larger ethos of the community. For those who could not be controlled through shaming or praise, traditional forms of control, corporal punishment was often seen as an alternative. The legal constraints placed on corporal punishment in the United States, however, left many of the informants baffled as is reflected in these two comments: 'There are too many restrictions on punishment here. You can't touch kids' (188/ASm); 'In the Philippines you could really punish kids; you knew their culture and customs. Parents give you permission to punish kids. In the US they (parents) would be waiting for you on the corner.' (189/ASf)

Overwhelming task and loss of face

Acknowledging the powerful role that teachers play in a child's life, and indeed that teachers had for most of them, the informants realized that: 'I will have a big effect if I do anything wrong.' (159/ASf) No one mentioned that the effect could possibly be positive. Rather than trivialize the discussions as reflecting a lack of self-esteem, the conversations more often were a testimony to the importance of teaching and teachers. Fear of making a mistake was motivated by the desire to 'do the right thing.' When they believed that they could not match up to this, the informants lapsed into musings such as these: 'I don't want to be responsible for the education of other people's children;' (166/ASf) 'I don't want to ruin a student's life.' (185/ASf)

'Losing face,' *diu mian* in Mandarin, the idea of being embarrassed or disgraced in front of someone else, is one of the most important concepts in Asian cultures. To laugh at someone's mistakes takes on a greater significance than humiliation. To many informants 'losing face' seemed inevitable in American classrooms and difficult to accept as part of a profession. As this young woman candidly revealed: 'We are afraid of being laughed at. Kids can be very mean.' (162/ASf) An Asian male went much further in his analysis of the complexity of surviving as a teacher within urban schools: 'There's too much freedom in America; students use freedom to intimidate the teacher.' (89/ASm) Throughout our discussion he continually weighed the benefits and costs of living in a less structured, less respectful society.

In order to counter kids' vindictiveness, teachers were perceived as needing to take on an intrusive role, one that was unnatural for Asian Americans. One young informant put it this way: 'Teachers have to be mean; they have to yell at kids.' (192/ASf) The required transformation of American teachers into aggressive combatants struggling to force students to listen and learn was seen as essential for this cultural context but as unacceptable within the Chinese model for a teacher. When the researcher suggested that teachers could also be nice, the informant came back forcefully: 'No, no, they [teachers] can't be; then they [students] will pick on you; I see this every day.' (174/ASf)

Separation of private and public selves

The sense of being overwhelmed by the demands of the profession related to the multiple responsibilities that a teacher is expected to assume, both for the children's academic lives and their emotional and social lives. In addition to subject matter, teachers must deal with the personal problems of students and their families. This expectation was more than most informants could see themselves meeting. They were stymied by the conflict they saw between the traditional role of teacher as expert in subject matter and the reality of teacher as negotiator between the often times opposing forces of home and school, society and culture, peers and family. As one informant bluntly claimed: 'I am not prepared to deal with crises in schools related to fighting, mediations, or rape.' (158/ASf)

To succeed in bridging some of these divides, teachers need strong inter-personal communication skills; they need to develop trust and a forum of open communication. This often translates into sharing of oneself with those outside of one's own kinship group. The majority of informants felt uncomfortable presenting their ideas or themselves to a strange audience. For many of the informants this was not only a difficult individual decision but also a major cultural reorientation. Often we heard that Asians not only do not like to talk in front of other people but also that they are not accus-tomed to talking about themselves, as explained by this young man: 'We don't talk about ourselves; we don't share with others.' (163/ASm) Although some may question this response as feeding a stereotype, many of the infor-mants claimed that indeed they, as a group, reflected many of the images that exist, perhaps not as individuals but as a cultural entity. The one that seemed to most work against the possibility of moving Asian Americans into public school teaching is exemplified in this powerful comment: 'Parents do not want kids to get involved with other people. Chinese do not get into other people's lives.' (157/ASf)

Language

As made clear in several interviews: 'Language is a major issue for Asians.' (161/ASf) The lack of English proficiency and the presence of accent played major roles in discouraging the informants from considering teaching as a career. Many perceived themselves unable to deal with the diversity of students from other cultures because they as Asian Americans either had limited English skills or would be perceived as having them. The preoccupa-tion with language as an obstacle to teaching took several forms. They feared making a mistake in modeling pronunciation for their students; they were concerned that students would misunderstand their meaning; and they saw limited fluency as an inhibition to fluid communication. They felt angered at an inability to speak their thoughts clearly and they cringed at the thought of possible ridicule. As one informant commented: 'There is no respect in the United States, especially for minorities with a language problem.' (175/ASf) It is for this reason, according to the informants, that many Asian Americans opt for careers that require math skills such as computers, engineering, science, and technology rather than those based on language skills. Lest these comments once again ring as stereotypes, we were reminded by several informants that: 'Few Asians challenge the stereotype of being quiet with an accent.' (190/ASm)

The Problematic Issue of High Standards Set by Chinese Traditions of Schooling

So what is the source of these attitudes that apparently cause the hesitancy toward, if not resistance to, teaching as a career? Ironically, the answer seemed to reside in Chinese culture itself, more specifically in the high regard for teaching and the standards set by Chinese culture for teachers. As one informant said: 'You have to think of yourself as a great person to be a teacher.' (188/ASf) In Japanese, the term *erai hito* explains this concept. This was not simply hesitancy on the part of youth who have not had adequate experience educating others; rather, informants claimed that the title of teacher had to be reserved for those who neared perfection. 'If there are ten qualities that a teacher needs and Chinese people do not meet all ten of those qualities, they will consider themselves not qualified to be a teacher' (156/ASf) or 'Young Asian people do not see themselves as good enough to be a teacher' (182/ASm) were comments sprinkled throughout the interviews. To tell others that you were interested in becoming a teacher verged on arrogance, not only because of the assumption that you were qualified beyond reproach, but also that you had the audacity to assume that you could teach other people's children to a standard that would be acceptable to Asian parents. As one young man said:

> Being a teacher means you have to be qualified. If I were to tell my parents that I wanted to be a teacher, they would laugh at me and say '*ne mo gee gok*' [Cantonese for 'you do not have the qualifications']. But in the American sense ... you don't have to be totally qualified because you learn as you teach. But in the Chinese way, you have to be perfect to teach.
>
> (157/ASm)

A related issue that compounds the hesitancy to declare an interest in teaching as a career and therefore risk losing the support of family and community, is the fear of failure. A young woman revealed: 'I am afraid to tell people that I want to be a teacher in case I fail.' (191/ASf) Combining the fear of losing face with the potential hubris in assuming the title of teacher, it is unsurprising that so few Asian Americans take the risky step into the field of teaching. Respect in the Chinese model is associated with structure, order, discipline, and reverence, all of which are dubious expectations for Asian Americans considering a career in teaching in America. The likelihood of entering a situation where respect is not conferred based on position but rather on performance frightened many of the informants. Some went so far as to claim that Asian Americans, as a cultural group, simply may be unsuited to the teaching profession:

It doesn't match our personality. We tend to be reserved people; we live a more sheltered life; we are not out-going people. Teachers must be out-going. We would be scared to be in a classroom as a young teacher. We like to have a small business, to do things on our own. Culturally we are not attracted to teaching as a profession.

(6/ASf)

This incongruity between the high expectations that Asians hold of teachers, as an outgrowth of respect for elders and learning, juxtaposed against the disrespectful realities of classrooms in America, played a major role in parental discouragement and, hence, resistance by Asian Americans to teaching as a career.

Concluding Remarks

The roadblocks for Asian Americans entering teaching varied greatly as seen by Asian American teachers and other informants in comparison with the previous racial groups discussed. Although Native Americans, African Americans, and Latinos often mentioned poor academic preparation and negative school experiences as possible contributing factors, this was not the case for the Asian American informants. In general, performance within the system is not a problem. What Asian Americans did share with other ethnic groups was the concern with image, respect, and the status of teaching as a career. They experienced the same discouragement from entering the profession from their community and families. The way this played out in the Asian context as seen from the previous commentary, however, was radically different.

6   On Race-matched Teaching

Most new teachers enter the profession with little, if any, preparation to address the diverse cultural and economic needs of urban youth (Little, 1989; Gougeon, 1993; Yee, 1990). Many teachers who currently work in inner-city public schools have been poorly selected, trained, and prepared for work in a multicultural context (Darling-Hammond and Sclan, 1996; Goodlad, et al., 1990; Spindler, 1987). In his paper, 'The "Melting Pot" Revisited', Wahab (1989) states that despite the flurry of commissions and reports on the shortage of minority teachers, little has been done to alter the way teachers are prepared to work with students from culturally diverse backgrounds. These reports include *A Nation Prepared: Teachers for the 21st Century*, issued by the Carnegie Foundation's Task Force on Teaching (Carnegie Forum on Education and the Economy, 1986) and *Tomorrow's Teachers* by the Holmes Group (1986), as well as others. The first report articulates the influence that the race and class of teachers have on students' attitudes toward school, society, and self. The second concludes that one of the main reasons students are not entering teaching is the decline in the professional status of the field. The reports' remedy is to provide career ladders based on higher degrees and passage of examinations.

Weiler (1988) and Apple (1986), seeing the gap that exists between the needs of teachers in multicultural classrooms and what is being offered on the 'reform' agenda, call for a teacher training program that would enable teachers to explore their own ethnocentric views and discuss issues of race and class. Montero-Sieburth (1989) agrees, contending that future teachers will need to be 'culturally sensitive and sensible' as well as skills-oriented and subject matter knowledgeable (p. 332). But is this enough? Several African American authors contend that there are particular qualities that exist within African American culture that can be best transmitted by other African Americans (Foster, 1994; Ladson-Billings and Henry, 1990). This idea of race-based teaching has led to the establishment of Africentric schools in communities across America (Hilliard, 1988; Asante, 1991) as well as efforts to recruit more African American students into teacher training.

Ethnocentric schools that focus on the history, culture, and literature of one's culture are not new. Within Asian communities throughout the world, overseas Chinese, Japanese, Koreans and, more recently, Vietnamese have gathered in separate ethnic-based schools either in lieu of public schooling or in addition to it. American and British schools are taken for granted in cities of all major nations. A common history, language, and world view, often in the face of oppression, provide subtle avenues of communication among a group of individuals who share a common heritage. At times what is transmitted to youth can appear to the dominant culture as racist or isolationist. Often the message is cloaked in stories of survival and resistance. Such ethnocentric philosophies are held by many groups, including Native Americans and Latinos. How these views are played out in the context of public schooling, however, varies. Although race-based teaching was supported by some African American, Native American and Latino teachers interviewed, it was almost totally absent from the Asian American interviews, with the exception of newly arrived Asian immigrants needing transitional language assistance.

African American Views

African American teachers held mixed views on race-matched teaching. Some claimed that you could understand 'your own kind' better and that there were certain kinds of knowledge that were more easily transmitted by Black teachers to Black children. Usually this had to do with 'racial uplift' and providing an awareness that 'you have to try twice as hard to get ahead.' Advocacy for race-matched teaching grows in part out of fear that teachers from other backgrounds, Whites in particular, will not provide equitable education to Black children. There is an assumption, based on historical realities, that African American children's behavior and demeanor might be misunderstood and that this ignorance will result in unfair treatment of Black children. While many of the Black teachers in this research claimed that African American children did indeed learn differently and, hence, required a different kind of disciplined learning environment, they also believed that perhaps parents might feel more comfortable if this discipline was provided by Black teachers: 'The Black community is more respectful of Black teachers than White. Black parents fear racism might enter into discipline. They think that Black teachers will be more fair. The more educated you are the more confident.' (52/AFf)

For others, the hesitancy to have Whites teach Black children came from the awareness that some White teachers are either afraid of African American children or give them too much latitude. Either way, both student and teacher lose. Students are not challenged academically and the teacher is not challenged professionally. White teachers were perceived as being soft on Black kids. They did not hold them accountable for their actions or their education in the same way that Black teachers could and would. Whites allowed African American children to get away with things. They made excuses for them, felt sorry for them, underestimated their abilities, didn't know how to work with them, or were just too lazy and didn't care. 'Black kids play games, tell middle-class White teachers what they want to hear, and White middle-class teachers fall for it; but Black teachers will call them on it.' (20/AFm)

African American teachers have traditionally perceived their responsibilities as extending into the community (Comer, 1988). Teachers who do not take the whole child into consideration and contend that their role is limited to teaching subject matter within the classroom are often perceived as selfish. When teaching for African Americans translates into connecting with a child's life, and the perception holds that Whites are unable or unwilling to do this, one can see how the following viewpoints might arise: 'Whites go into the classroom to move up' (27/AFf); 'Whites talk to children, not with them' (37/AFm); 'We minority teachers naturally teach all children but White teachers don't have the experience. They don't understand.' (76/AFf) Again, what is important is not whether these statements are true or not, but that they are freely and openly expressed. They become a part of the folk wisdom of the community.

Since the majority of United States teachers are White, middle-class females, an understandable cultural clash can occur if they are unprepared for the social and economic realities of children who do not come from the same class, racial, and language background (Hale-Benson, 1982). Although this may be true, Henry and Jackson's research showed that this lack of preparation for work in urban schools is not simply race-based. 'Culture shock and low self-esteem from working in an urban school can also be experienced by minority teachers, whose life experiences more closely approximate those of the White middle-class' (Henry and Jackson quoted in Grant and Secada, 1989, p. 765).

Many of the interviews echoed Henry and Jackson's findings. Although some of the informants in this research believed that teachers of color were better at handling students of color, the vast majority admitted to being at a loss as to how to work with inner-city youth. For some, the reason was lack of exposure to large school systems: 'I came from a small town in Ohio and then to Cincinnati. I was frightened internally, I believed ill-equipped' (48/AFf); 'Cincinnati was my first urban experience. I was in a small town before [in Florida]. I have very little in common with, or understanding of, poor urban kids. I wasn't raised that way.' (40/AFf) Others admitted that, although they might have been poor during their childhood in the South, they were raised with a very strong sense of self-respect and community, something they found lacking in the North and West: 'I came to Detroit; it frightened me, coming from a small Southern town. I've never lived in a ghetto, in the South we were just poor.' (43/AFf) Still others were from middle-class, highly educated families and did not see urban children as part of their community: 'I wasn't trained for the inner city. I never experienced some of the things that these kids live.' (39/AFm)

Similarly, a teacher of 'minority' status is not necessarily equipped to teach other children of 'minority' status, especially if they have different ethnic, language, and cultural heritages. The assumption that any person of color can handle any child of color has led to unnecessary difficulties and misunderstanding. In the Long Beach School District this was made poignantly clear. Many African American teachers who had been hired with the understanding that they could work with 'minority' children were at a loss in dealing with Latino, Cambodian, Laotian, and Samoan students. A few were taking courses on their own to find out about these cultures and languages. Because of this lack of preparation, teachers were struggling to find ways to engage and educate an increasingly diverse school population. The issues do not divide up along color lines as reflected in these comments:

> You don't have to be Black to teach Blacks. Every teacher has to be versatile; you do what is best for different groups of students. Some teachers are very naive. One needs to see that just because one is poor, it doesn't mean that someone is stupid. We shouldn't make assumptions based on race and culture. It's very hard to get rid of a belief such as racism. How can people with small minds teach others about the world? There are other communities that are growing and are not being addressed, like Cambodian, Samoan, etc. Teachers have many false assumptions about these other cultures.
>
> (16/AFf)

Some informants actually believed that to be a Black teacher in a Black school was to their disadvantage. Differences in socioeconomic class and age seemed to contribute to this view. Several cited examples where racism had been internalized to the extent that some Black children and their parents believed Black teachers were inferior to Whites. Others extended this analysis to a supposition that because most Blacks were victims of lower quality educational systems, Black teachers were not as qualified and, therefore, less desirable in terms of educating the next generation. The criticism of Black teachers being viewed as too traditional, conservative, and demanding also echoed through the interviews. The conundrum was illuminated in this conversation: 'White kids won't listen to me because I'm Black. They assume I'm stupid and lack respect. And Black kids won't listen to me because I'm Black; it has to do with denigration and self-hate. They'll listen to a White teacher more because of higher status.' (38/AFf)

Within the African American community the traditional view of education highlights the importance of partnership between school and home with reinforcement coming from the community and the church. Black middle-class flight from cities has left urban schools and their constituents isolated from middle-class role models, jobs and opportunities; it has also left urban teachers isolated from their students and their families (Delpit, 1988). What teachers know of their students is often limited to the narrow confines of the classroom. They know little of their other life skills and responsibilities to their family, their church or community. As one elderly gentleman explained:

> Teachers are so removed from the area in which they teach; they don't see things in the community. They don't have to live in the community. That's a choice. If it's a job, you can leave, but if it's a profession, you must stay. On Saturday in the grocery store my kids [students] bag my groceries. On Sunday, they're in church. Teachers need to see students in other roles and they need to see you. They see me in my yard, they know where I live.
>
> (88/AFm)

The result is that in most urban school districts there is little community identity or contact. Teachers who used to live in the same community as they teach now commute long distances from their homes in the suburbs. Many of these teachers claim that they have the right to live where they want, to be a participant in the benefits of the middle class, to send their children to whatever schools they wish. As reinforced by one angry, veteran teacher: 'Minorities from the middle class are going to the suburbs because they think that teaching is more effective there; it's a myth.' (37/AFm) Whether it is true or not, the point is that we cannot assume that African American teachers can, or indeed want to, identify with the needs of inner-city, low-income African American youth. Although the sharing of a common experience of racism in this country often overrides other salient aspects of individual identity, the historical, economic, cultural and educational context of teachers' lives inevitably influences how they view themselves, their options, and their profession. Freedom of choice over location of employment, place of residence, and quality of lifestyle must be honored.

Latino Views

The exponential growth in the Latino and Southeast Asian school-age population in Southern California has forced school districts, such as the one in Long Beach, to critically assess how to best prepare teachers to work with students whose background may not match their own. Given the growing numbers of Latino students who continue to leave school prior to graduation, it should come as no surprise that the informants were emphatic about the need for teachers who are both aware of, and capable of responding to, the multiple needs of Latino children. Teachers were clear that this was not a simple matter of having more teachers who spoke Spanish. Many of the students who are failing in the system are native speakers of English. Of utmost concern to these teachers was the inability of many educators to differentiate among the various ethnic groups that make up the arbitrary category, 'Hispanic' or 'Latino.' Without an understanding of the complexity of ethnicities and how they are mediated through socioeconomic class, color, educational opportunities, and regionalism, teachers are bound to mislabel and misrepresent their students, resulting in profound inequities. One bilingual teacher went to great length to clarify the situation:

> There are major differences between ILI, those who have never gone to school, the illiterates, [it is difficult for them to even sit in a chair or hold a pencil] and ELD, those who have gone to school in their native language and need to be able to transfer skills into English. Unfortunately, these children are lumped together because of their lack of facility with English, and the standards are geared down. Students who could be performing at college prep level are given worksheets or taught study skills.
>
> (7/LAf)

She continued to explain the two kinds of Mexican American students who dominate the Long Beach school system:

> First, there are those who come to America from low-socioeconomic standing in Mexico. Usually their parents have not been educated past the third grade. Since there is no compulsory education in Mexico for all children, they see education as a luxury. When there is difficulty at home, the child is expected to miss school and help out. If the child acts up in school, the parent disciplines the child by keeping the child at home. Sometimes they will return to Mexico for extended periods. They may have a job that pays minimum wage that is more important for survival than school.
>
> Then there are those who are from educated families in Mexico. They may have been in private schools receiving a better education than their peers here in America. But when they come to America and enter school they are usually put in ESL/ELD classes, especially if they are high school students. These classes are devoid of content [and instead are] focusing on the rudimentary aspects of language acquisition, for example, naming parts of the body or objects in a room.
>
> After two periods a day of such boring work, these teenagers are placed in regular classrooms where they are unable to understand the

subject matter in English. Some of these students have already studied physics and economics in their own language in Mexico. In America their education stops. They could continue with subject matter taught in Spanish. This is true for Vietnamese, Japanese and other cultures as well.

(7/LAf)

It was her contention that it is the latter group of Latino students that need the most attention because they come to this country with extensive cultural capital upon which they could build. If they drop out of school because of boredom or redundancy, the Latino middle class will lose its most essential resource: the development of its youth for future leadership positions.

The assumption that persons of the same ethnicity could teach their own better than could persons from outside of the specific ethnic grouping drew angry responses from several of the Latino informants. One male despaired: 'The educational community makes a mistake in assuming that minorities can handle their own better than Whites.' (1/LAm) Another commented: 'Just because you're a minority it doesn't mean that you know how to work with kids. Sometimes it can be worse if you're a minority and a bad teacher. Kids will say, "I don't want to grow up like her/him." The difficulty is that there are so few minorities [in teaching].' (86/LAm and Lebanese)

Given that the Latino teachers interviewed spanned a range of ethnicities including Cuban, Mexican, Nicaraguan, and Honduran, a range of viewpoints might be expected. But even within any of these ethnic backgrounds a host of variables emerged that these teachers assumed resided within their students since it was clearly a part of their own identity as adults. The assumption that speaking Spanish or having a Spanish surname automatically gave you access and knowledge of 'Latino culture' sparked many animated conversations. A Latina spoke from her own frustration:

It's not true that you can handle minority kids if you are a minority. My culture is very bicultural. We were never Catholic. Two of my sisters are Jewish, the other two are Mormons. All seven of us are teachers. But just because I speak Spanish doesn't mean that I know the customs.

(102/LAf)

Inquiring as to how to determine if certain individuals have the qualifications necessary to work with such diversity led one Latino informant to exclaim: 'Some people never will be able to teach minorities. It doesn't mean that they are racist, but they just can't relate to them. They need exposure and experience with people of color.' (86/LAm and Lebanese) The story that he then related further complicated the situation as he clearly did not draw a clear demarcation line between Whites and people of color. Over the next few minutes he went into great detail to explain the many times he has had to intervene on behalf of African American students because of their maltreatment by a Latina librarian.

As was true in every ethnic group, the most difficulty came when teachers and students clashed along socioeconomic lines. Teachers from middle-class and upper-middle-class families often resented having to work with low-income, low-status children. In the interviews reported here, the hostility proved most prominent when the mix combined Cuban upper-middle-class teachers with Mexican migrant kids. The reverse situation also occurred, however, where Mexican teachers who had not had access to higher education were working with Latino children whose cultural capital far exceeded their own. The parents of these middle-class children were appalled by the low quality of language used, the low expectations, and lack of rigor provided for their children.

Some of the interviews with middle-class Latina/o teachers proved painful as they critically and harshly judged the students in their charge. I flinched at comments that would have been construed as racist if said by someone of another ethnicity. As an ethnographer I tried to see such attitudes as yet one more manifestation of impediments that working-class Latino youth face in their sojourn through the system. Given that these were inner-city schools and that many of the teachers were of middle-class status, there is a strong likelihood that, although of the same perceived ethnicity, their alliances were not with these children.

When I asked about links between community and schools, the responses were similarly mixed. Although several teachers acknowledged the problem of middle-class flight, seeing such a movement as robbing the community and, hence, its children, of professional role models, others were indignant in their claims that they had the right to live whereever they pleased. These latter teachers claimed that they did not feel any special responsibility to the community in which they taught. This was particularly true if the school was in the inner city. One woman, in particular, took offense; but her attitude was shared by others: 'I don't live in this area and I don't want to.' (13/LAm) In fact, some teachers believed that the assumption that they should live in the inner city was one of the very barriers to students of color opting to become teachers.

Native American Views

Having more Native teachers and administrators working with Native youth might appear as a possible answer to encouraging more Native teachers but it was not seen as a priority among the Indian teachers interviewed. The reasoning was complex. Throughout the conversations with teachers in both ethnocentric Native American schools, which attempt to instill pride in culture, and urban public schools who have Native students, the responses to race-matched teaching were mixed. In general, the goal of the vast majority of Native teachers, as was true of the Latino informants, was to find individuals who would commit to providing fair and equitable education for their children regardless of ethnicity. They did not assume that only Native teachers could teach Native children.

Whether the resistance to encouraging more Native people to go into teaching was based on the assumption of dilution of culture and loss of self or whether the reality that being Native did not guarantee that you could or would provide the best education to Native children was unclear. They knew about intertribal rivalry, hierarchy within tribes, and the difficulties that their own people had faced in acquiring schooling. On the one hand, they wanted access to the knowledge that would free their people from poverty and subservience; on the other hand, they did not want to give up cultural traditions that made them Indian in order to become acceptably professional. How schools, or if schools, could help in bridging this gap was under debate. For now, the focus centered on the need to increase all teachers' understanding of the complexity of what might constitute 'Native culture and traditions.'

Asian American Views

Paradoxically, although Asian American teachers and other Asian informants claimed that they would not be as good at teaching a child whose cultural background differed from their own, they largely dismissed any benefit that an Asian child might gain from being taught by an Asian teacher. Nearly all of the non-teacher informants failed to see race-matched teaching as valuable or necessary and thus not a motive for their joining the teaching force. In response to 'Would you have liked more Asian teachers and would this have made a difference?,' the overwhelming majority said that Asian teachers would be useful only as translators for immigrants who needed assistance in transitioning to American life. Once students grasped the basics of English, the important factor became quality of pedagogy not ethnic background. One young informant expressed it this way: 'I never had an Asian teacher. I had good teachers who treated me like everyone else. They didn't discriminate.' (183/ASf)

Several of the informants were visibly upset by the thought of race-matched teaching, fearing that Asian teachers would reach out to Asian students in a different way, thereby stigmatizing, isolating, or favoring those students. They believed that Asian teachers would be biased towards them and, hence, give them more attention than they wanted or deserved. (6/ASf) The focus was on *not* wanting special assistance or consideration. One could argue that this supports the Japanese saying, *Deru kui wa utareru,* 'A tall tree catches much wind,' but it could also be based on the desire simply to be accepted as American, not as different or unusual. This desire to be 'normal,' to fit in, seemed inherent in Asian informants' wanting their children educated by individuals from a wide range of backgrounds. One Vietnamese American commented: 'We want to broaden our knowledge by learning from different types of people. We are eager to have our children integrated into American society so they can function well.' (172/ASm)

Perhaps because of this variation across linguistic cultures as well as the desire to move effectively and efficiently into mainstream American culture, Asian American teachers and other informants saw little use for primary language instruction in public schools. They claimed to misunderstand the demands being made by the Latino community for bilingual education. The Asian American view was 'We can do this at home. I don't see it as the state's responsibility to teach [my language].' (89/ASm) Language, as a part of culture, was something that came from the home and family and was reinforced by the community. Schooling, on the other hand, was about learning skills for success and survival in American society. Although operating in separate domains, the one did not preclude the other.

As a result, the support for bilingual education among Asian Americans was mixed. Some of the informants claimed that their experience in bilingual classes or ESL classes had benefited them. It provided them with the decoding skills necessary to comprehend their new country more quickly. Others were angry that such classes 'did not use English enough and therefore delayed [their] access [to the dominant language].' (163/ASf) Several conversations highlighted the problems of misplacement in bilingual classes. Pilipino students were placed in Spanish-speaking classes because of the Spanish derivation of their surnames even though they had never spoken a word of Spanish in their lives and saw their primary identity as Asian. Students from Hong Kong whose first language is English and second language Cantonese sat for months alongside Mandarin-speaking students ignorant of the buzz of sounds and tones surrounding them. Southeast Asians were often seen as a homogenous group rather than from distinct countries with radically different cultural, religious, and linguistic traditions.

The perception that a teacher of the same race would naturally enhance, favor, or increase demands on a child of the same ethnicity, although intimated by individuals in other ethnic groups, was usually seen by most teachers of color in a positive light. Only with Asian Americans did it take on a more sinister aspect. The majority of Asian Americans actually expressed a desire to *not* be educated by a teacher whose ancestry was identified as Asian. Asian teachers were viewed as more traditional and stricter; they limited young people's freedom to grow and express themselves. Some of the informants related negative experiences with Asian teachers. One concluded that she would not have wanted more: 'They were too Chineseee (sic); they expected too much.' (188/ASf) Others scoffed at the idea that matching two people of 'Asian' background could improve one's education or comfort level in the classroom. Perhaps because of the complexity of ethnicities reflected in the term 'Asian' and the geographic and historical realities for the peoples involved, a hierarchical foundation of mistrust remains. Would Korean parents accept the discipline of their child by a Japanese teacher? Or a Cambodian child the constraint by a Vietnamese teacher? Even when of the same ethnicity within American racial categories, problems can and do arise such as between Taiwanese teachers and Mainland Chinese students. Differences in class, culture, and parental status both educationally and financially further complicate the picture. One young man critically interrogated the whole assumption around race-matched teaching in cynically inquiring: 'What could a Cambodian refugee possibly have in common with a third-generation Japanese? That they are both "Asian"?' (169/ASm)

Concluding Remarks

The basic belief underlying race-based role modeling is that 'Minority teachers can relate better to minority children.' (20/AFm) If we follow this contention, there is an even greater urgency to increase the number of teachers of color. Such an assumption, however, leaves us with numerous questions: Do children learn better from people most like themselves? If so, should Latino teachers be expected to teach only Latino children? Are African American teachers less able to teach European American kids? Do we select and train teachers differently depending on the clientele? Do students of one skin color learn differently from students with another color within the meanings of color provided by a culture? Or are there other issues involved that at times can override coloration? According to the teachers of color interviewed, socioeconomic status and exposure to inner-city kids deeply inform teacher attitudes as to whom they want to teach and how they teach. The educational and professional background of family, type of schooling received, immigrant status, time in country, regionalism, and even age further complicate the shaping of these teacher attitudes.

Haberman (1987) astutely notes that minority individuals who have succeeded and are making progress from compulsory schooling into pre-professional programs have survived not only the tracking process of school but also the screening of higher education. Many of those who have done both are often from middle-class families, have attended predominantly White schools, have difficulty identifying with inner-city minority culture, and have little desire to teach in urban schools. Perhaps the real question becomes: Can we prepare teachers to work with diversity that is not within their comfort level? I would contend that, yes, we can; but any analysis is incomplete without an understanding of the multiple factors that play into one's success as a teacher in urban schools.

7   Reforming Teacher Education

The interviews for this research provided me with a unique opportunity to hear from numerous teachers of color their views on how to best prepare *all* teachers to work with students from diverse economic, ethnic, and linguistic backgrounds. Most of the teachers in all three urban school districts began their responses highly critical of current teacher education programs. The need to vent their frustration and anger appeared to be a prerequisite to their willingness to make constructive suggestions for change. The three main criticisms included: lack of encouragement or support while in teacher education programs, lack of practical training in teacher education programs, and lack of preparation to work with diversity. After listening to their concerns, we will be better able to hear their recommendations. Please note that in this chapter and the one that follows the recommendations are not separated out by ethnicity other than the numbered identifier after each quotation. As suggestions for change, the tone is much more linear and dogmatic, asking that we listen to these veteran teachers with minimal commentary and analysis. That will come later.

Criticism of Teacher Education Programs

According to the majority of informants, traditional methods of training teachers are no longer adequate for the needs of today's children. Teacher education programs and their faculties were heavily criticized for a lack of awareness of, and detachment from, public schools. Many informants considered their training in colleges of education as a waste of time; some even saw it as detrimental. A recurring criticism of teacher education programs was that they were too theoretical and did not relate to the reality of the classrooms. The typical program of a year of theory prior to a few weeks of student teaching was seen as a farce. Although I have heard university professors dismiss this criticism as a desire on the part of teachers to water down the pre-service curriculum, the teachers put it differently: 'University teacher education was [training] for upper-class suburban areas; it was a waste. You have to develop your own method once in schools. You need classes on drug, alcohol, and child abuse, more counseling courses' (39/AFm); 'What I learned in university had nothing to do with the classroom. It was too theoretical; it would never work in schools. The faculty have no idea of the interpersonal skills necessary' (38/AFf); 'The teacher education process is too complicated. One half is not necessary. Put in more practical. Academics are not so important. The prerequisites should be the desire to work with kids' (42/AFm); 'It was all busy work. I was disgusted with the program. I became a teacher in spite of my teacher training experience' (97/ASf); 'Teacher education was always a mystery to me. A lot of what I took in education courses I already learned in other humanities and science courses in high school. It was common sense. What is the purpose of teacher education anyway?' (103/AFm)

According to many of these teachers, minimal support and limited practical experience result in teachers beginning their professional careers unprepared. This is particularly true when they are placed in urban settings and expected to work with children from diverse ethnic, linguistic, and economic backgrounds. Some inner-city veteran teachers among the informants have actually given up accepting student teachers because of the naive assumptions with which students leave colleges. On the other side of this equation, fewer and fewer colleges of education are placing their future teachers in urban settings, preferring to put them in 'exemplary schools' or PDSs (professional development schools) (Schlechty, et al., 1989). Either way, low-income children of color lose by not having their teachers prepared and able to work with their individual needs.

Recommendations for Changes in Teacher Education

Over half of the informants recommended that the major change needed in teacher education programs was to involve students in a variety of school and community settings early in their undergraduate experience. Other suggestions included: involve parents, prepare teachers to work with diversity, prepare educators to train teachers, increase the range of pedagogical skills to work with diverse student populations, increase understanding of the social, economic, and political realities of the profession, require seminar-style lab classes, and increase access to, and support in, college.

Involve students in a variety of school and community settings early in their undergraduate experience

Early exposure to school classrooms was seen not only as advantageous for the future teacher's understanding of the complexity of the teaching profession, but also as a right, a courtesy, so that students can find out at the start if this is the career for them or not. Considering that more than half of those who graduate from teacher education programs do not choose to become teachers, it would appear advantageous as well as cost-effective to examine the role early involvement could play in the lives of potential teachers. As one teacher pointed out, kids suffer when individuals become teachers simply because they have already invested the time and money. The following comments illuminated the problem: 'I can't think of a greater tragedy than to have a student go through four years of teacher education and not have classroom experience, then find out that they don't like it' (54/AFf); 'Student teaching should be at the beginning, so they can see if they are cut out for it. There are many teachers who shouldn't be teaching. They didn't find out soon enough. It's the kids that suffer.' (7/LAf)

In addition to early involvement, twenty percent of the informants emphasized the need for experiences in a variety of school and community settings with internships for two or three years in a variety of schools. Acknowledging the shock that new teachers experience when going from a middle-class to a working-class school, one African American male teacher laid out his justification for a similar plan:

> One quarter of observation is ludicrous. One semester of student teaching locks you into one teacher. There's too much pressure of grades hanging over their heads. My idea would be to have one full year in four different school environments, to observe all types of classes, no responsibilities. Then one year of cadet teaching; one-half semester with top students and one-half with lower-end students. Then two years of community experience before certification. Most teachers have no exposure to the real world.
>
> (88/AFm)

About ten percent of the informants believed that it was imperative that future teachers have at least one student-teaching assignment working with students of color in an inner-city situation. Informants questioned the current trend to place future teachers only in 'the best schools':

> Teachers need more bad and good experience. Teachers fall apart when they hit a difficult experience. Being Black I had an edge, I could understand where they were coming from. Inner-city experience should be mandatory, also a first-generation middle-income school, then an upper-class school.
>
> (52/AFf)

'Put student teachers in difficult urban areas, otherwise they're lost. Expose them to the classroom early. They need to see Black teachers' (64/AFf); 'Require an experience in an inner-city school. If they can work in inner-city they can work anywhere.' (46/AFf)

Involve parents

Directly connected to the recommendation to increase the involvement of future teachers in a variety of classroom and community settings early in their undergraduate experience was the desperate outcry for training to work with parents. Fifteen percent of the informants expressed great anxiety about their inability to work with parents. One has to remember that we are not talking here about White teachers trying to relate to 'minority' parents; all the informants are 'minorities' themselves. However, each of the teachers interviewed is unique and entered the profession with her or his own set of values, be they regional, religious, or socioeconomic. Since these values varied among the informants of the same ethnic group, not to mention between groups, it should be of no surprise that they might also differ from those of the parents of the children they taught. This became particularly apparent as I became more aware of the fact that about half of the informants admitted to being unprepared to work with inner-city parents and in some cases fearing them.

Because of the significant role that parents play in the lives of children, the informants highly recommended that all future teachers be trained in the skills necessary to work well with parents, including interviewing procedures and how to hold a parent conference. Here are some of their suggestions and justifications for such training:

> Parents from low income are turned off to education. They feel guilty; they're busy. The most intimidating part of my job is parents. Maybe we need to get future teachers in contact with teachers who work well with parents. Have parents express their concern to these future teachers. We need workshops.
>
> (79/LAf)

> There have to be classes [in teacher education programs] on dealing with parents; helping low self-esteem. Parents do not have confidence in schools. They don't want to come to school and face teachers. They feel poorly in manners, dress, and speaking in American society. Parents feel inferior. We need to know a lot more about the people, so we can reach the parents.
>
> (7/LAf)

Prepare teachers to work with diversity

Training teachers to work with parents and the community means preparing teachers to work with diversity. Over one-third of the informants noted that all teachers need better preparation in working with inner-city students. This need was expressed not only for future teachers but for veteran teachers who have never had the training. Three general areas of discussion dominated the recommendations: do not assume that minorities are responsible for educating their own people; ignorance of cultural differences is hurting students; and provide multicultural education for all teachers.

Many of the informants took issue with the dominant view that we need more minority teachers to teach their own people: 'You can't expect minorities to only teach minorities.' A Southeast Asian American teacher lamented:

> Most teachers are not prepared to teach in a multicultural/multilingual setting. There is ignorance about the Vietnam war. They ask me if I'm from the North or the South. Americans must learn from other cultures. Refugees need their culture understood.
>
> (89/ASm)

A Latina echoed this urgency in relationship to her own people: 'All teachers need this sort of training (bilingual). Teachers need to get to know the culture, the psychology of Hispanics, where they are coming from.' (7/LAf) Two African American women detailed their concern: 'Student teachers are not prepared to work with diversity or the classroom. Black English is OK. You can't assume that they are stupid. It is not a sign of belligerence; it's a dialect' (38/AFf); 'Behaviors based on culture are perceived as off-task, discipline problems. We need to acknowledge differences and be sensitive to culture.' (50/AFf) Another offered some suggestions:

> I don't see color. If you can work with Black kids you can work with anyone. Black kids appear angry but they're not. What's up? Don't take it personally. A lot of teachers 'name clip'. We should save face for kids not the teacher. Don't hold grudges. It's ok to lose fights but not control. Be authentic, don't try to be what you're not; be fair.
>
> (24/AFf)

A recent young graduate, commenting on the inadequate preparation that teachers receive to work in multicultural classrooms, exploded: 'In the College of Education we were taught methods courses to deal with the "average child." They didn't prepare us for diverse children. "At-risk" wasn't even in the vocabulary.' (75/ASf) This lack of attention to the needs of diverse students prompted a discussion on the need for mentoring for all teachers. This often translated into a long term buddy system to prevent isolation and provoke free flow of questions and suggestions. The importance of having someone to share ideas and experiences without judgement had significant currency among these veteran teachers, as seen in this comment: 'Minority teachers need help by other minority teachers, shadowing. They can tell you that you can expect this to happen, but don't take it personally, keep going.' (23/ASf) The extension could be made that with a sense of greater competency and comfort, teachers would exude an enthusiasm for their work that could ignite a student's interest in academics and perhaps in teaching itself.

Prepare educators to train teachers

Two immediate ways to get at the problem of the shortage of minority faculties in colleges and schools of education as well as address the lack of awareness of the needs of a multicultural school population are to require college faculty participation in schools and engage clinical practitioners in the training of future teachers. Twenty percent of the informants questioned the integrity and ability of faculty members who claim to train teachers for today's classrooms:

> Professors tend not to know what goes on in the classroom. If they were in [school] classrooms more, they could impart this knowledge to their students; this would be helpful, especially if they could provide answers to real problems, like having too many students combined with special education and Chapter I [federal legislative designation]. There are six years of difference in ability in some classes. How do you do 'cooperative learning' with these students? Some can't recognize their own name. Faculty need to get out of their middle-class views.
>
> (12/AFf)

Having university faculties participating in the public schools was not only seen as an asset for preparing future teachers, but such involvement would improve the quality of and enthusiasm for teaching on the part of professors themselves. Seeing faculty members of colleges of education as a potential source of clarifying cultural differences for future teachers, one Native American informant commented:

> Faculty should participate in the community, go on to the reservation. People don't understand the differences between the various types of Indians, how diverse and rich our culture is. They think that we are all Plains Indians.
>
> (111/NAf)

Several teacher informants spoke earnestly about the need to prepare future teachers better to the point of wanting to participate in the training of future teachers themselves. Many of these statements were based on a willingness to sacrifice their own time to assist in the training, so great was their fear that the students being produced by colleges of education could do more damage than good in urban schools. These comments reveal their concern: 'I would do anything to insure that quality teachers will continue to take my place after I have retired' (53/AFf); 'Yes, I think that I would take on the extra load to help future teachers be better prepared' (53/AFf); 'I would love to be able to assist in training future teachers.' (84/AFf)

Increase the range of pedagogical skills to work with diverse school populations

A recurring irritation expressed by the informants throughout the interviews was the lack of awareness on the part of college faculties of the role that discipline plays in teaching. Ten percent of the informants blamed teacher education programs for sacrificing future teachers to schools without class-room management training. Although one might dispute the extent to which pre-service courses should focus their attention on classroom management, the need for training in interpersonal skills was most pronounced.

Comments from a half-dozen informants suggested training in ways to build trust and respect between student and teacher and among students. Some informants believed that until this step had been taken, learning would not take place, especially for working-class minority children. As this young African American woman learned early in her career:

> If you don't have kids' respect, then you can't teach them. Kids' percep-tion of you is very important. Teachers send off fears and confusion. Teacher as messenger; this is important to understand. Teachers need the flexibility and the ability to respond to change.
>
> (38/AFf)

An Asian American teacher agreed: 'They must respect the teacher first, then they will listen to what you say. We need to teach teachers to teach values. We need teachers who are charismatic, who feel committed. Once the seed is planted, kids will flourish.' (75/ASf) A Native teacher took the issue of respect one step further: 'Teach them that life is not just based on money; emphasize values. Native American values go against the dominant culture, but they are important; they should be respected and listened to.' (113/NAf) An African American male, alluding to the importance of community in his education, eloquently expounded: 'Teachers need to know how to build a family out of a classroom; respect one another. Love is most important for minority kids. The child has to feel love before [she] can learn.' (94/AFm)

In most cases, what teachers referred to in calling for increased classroom management skills was, in fact, the lack of strong pedagogical skills. It is interesting that when the latter is missing, it is easy to see the student as an adversary, as something that one does something to, that needs managing. One informant offered some guidance:

> Not everyone who is a specialist is a good teacher. Emphasis needs to be on knowing how to teach rather than on the amount of knowledge in a

particular field. College of education courses need to teach you how to take ideas and break them down for children of diverse value systems, how to be creative, how to keep the kids with you. How to take a concept and teach it to all children.

(75/ASf)

Increase understanding of the social, economic, and political realities of the profession

Ten percent of the informants addressed the need for colleges of education to equip future teachers better for the realities of the classroom through coursework dealing with the concerns of urban youth. Through the study of social issues, teachers might better understand the historical, economic, and cultural basis for their students' responses to the educational environment and to them personally. Related to this theme was the conviction that it was about time that the 'truth' be told and in doing so everyone would benefit. A more honest account of the sources of racial and economic inequities would provide teachers and students with an historical context in which to view present time differences.

The recommendations calling for a greater awareness of what the profession holds in store for the newly initiated teacher included the suggestion that future teachers become acquainted with the overall ecology of the school. This often translated as learning about what the administration's job was and how the individual teacher related to the overall decision-making process within the building. Some informants criticized and questioned the role of the administration. Others just wished that principals would pay a bit more attention to what they as teachers did. It was common to hear that a principal had not come into a classroom to observe teaching for an entire year. One second-year African American woman lamented: 'I need more control in my classroom. I sometimes feel that the administration doesn't care what I do. I feel like a student. We need more contact with administrators. I still don't know how the school system works.' (38/AFf) This harks back to the need for mentoring of new teachers and the problem of isolation in the classroom. But it also reflects the lack of adequate exposure to the political realities of schooling through internships in urban school settings as well as through the academic curriculum in teacher education programs.

Require seminar-style lab classes

Throughout the interviews the idea of using lab classes as a means to improve the quality of college classroom teaching kept popping up. Although it had many forms, the basic idea was that problems and issues would be brought in from the field and discussed in small groups: 'Use case

studies and ask future teachers, "What would you do in this situation."'
(69/AFf) The lab classes could include mini-teaching sessions, case studies,
critiquing of peer work, and exploration of controversial issues. Several of
the teachers believed that, 'Peer-training is important' (59/AFm); 'Have
them teach their peers. Tell future teachers that they must become the peak
of "studentness."' Tell them, 'You, as future teachers, have to model the type
of student that you would want to be in your class when you are a teacher.
Give them time for reflection. Challenge them.' (106/ASm & E.Indian)

Increase access to and support in college

Approximately ten percent of the informants noted that colleges and universities could increase the participation rate of students of color in teacher
education programs by providing greater access to higher education and
support once there. A Latino science teacher criticized teacher education
programs in addressing the perceived lack of hospitality often experienced
by first-generation college students. From his perspective:

> The teacher education program at [XX] was really discouraging. They
> beat you up at the doorway. The counselor's first words were 'you're not
> going to make it' even though I had a 3.3 GPA [grade point average].
> You really have to want to be a teacher to survive. I was not an isolated
> case. A friend of mine who is mulatto and has a BA from Harvard got
> the same treatment [here at XX].
>
> (86/LAm & Lebanese)

Advocacy for open admissions to teacher education programs with on-
going support proved popular among several of the informants, perhaps
because many of them knew people who would have been great teachers
had they been able to gain access to, and survive the pressures and alienation of, college. Some went so far as to recommend: 'Accept everyone into
the program; let experience decide who stays.' (53/AFf) Others claimed that
low grades keep some potentially good teachers out: 'Give kids with lower
grades a chance to see what they can do on the job. Some people are
looking for a purpose in a job; we've lost good teachers due to low GPA'
(76/AFf)

Once in college, students need support, especially first-generation college
students of color who are attending predominantly White institutions. The
informants were fully aware of the need for tutoring, mentoring, and moni-
toring. An Asian American male teacher shared how he and his classmates
survived:

> We had a Vietnamese club to help our own people. I was president; I
> matched upperclassmen with underclassmen. Everything was explained

in both Vietnamese and English. We couldn't have made it otherwise. Undergraduate tutoring is essential.

(32/ASm)

Knowing of the numerous Latino students who have fallen through the cracks once in college, one Latino teacher advocated a much stronger system of accountability and advisement: 'we need some kind of system where you constantly monitor the people going through [college].' (13/LAm) Although this might appear oppressive to some people, in my prior research on the value of minority culture-based programming for students of color on college campuses, an honest account of where you stood and what you needed to do to survive was seen as liberating, not stifling (Gordon, 1997a).

8 Recommendations for Recruiting Students of Color into the Profession

As we look at recommendations for increasing the actual numbers of minority youth choosing careers in teaching, we must identify solutions for all aspects of the problems facing students of color as they move through schooling and compete for careers. After all, professional careers are going to continue to be available only on a competitive basis. The skills needed for eventual success must be acquired early in their educational lives, along with the motivation to face the often inhospitable confines of college and graduate study. Clearly, we need to increase the levels of achievement for African American, Latino, and Native American students beginning in the early grades and continuing through college (Vegas, et al., 1998). We also need, however, to seek ways to make the teaching profession attractive to students of color so that all groups are eventually more represented in future class rooms. This chapter provides us with recommendations and insights from the interviews with urban teachers on how to address all aspects of the situation affecting the future supply of teachers of color for US schools. The recommendations follow a developmental flow beginning with attempts to enhance educational success and arouse interest in teaching as a career through the improvement of school education and the image of teaching.

Children incorporate into their dreams for a future the images and hopes that adults hold for them. Community conversations about teaching as well as commentary by teachers themselves pertaining to their profession profoundly affect how children view their career options. Relationships with people who have succeeded within the system aid in the attitudinal changes so important for the motivation to stay in school. Recruitment to college depends on school performance. Once in college, students need clear advisement that moves them into strong majors that can support entrance to teacher education programs. Throughout their undergraduate college years, coursework that introduces them to the complexity of schooling, in combination with first-hand experience in schools, particularly with low-income children, would aid in both self-selection and preparation for the teaching profession. Students who then decide to go into teaching need to realize that as a professional the learning does not stop upon graduation.

Recommendations for Recruiting Students of Color

As the teachers in this study revealed, in order to keep abreast of the profession and to be effective with youth from all walks of life, further education and practical training throughout one's career are essential. As one reads through these recommendations, it is interesting to reflect on how the emphasis shifts from concern with higher pay to the importance of practical involvement in the lives of children and their families. It would behoove us to listen to these recommendations, particularly in light of the often misguided recruitment efforts made on behalf of students of color.

Improve school education

The reality of students' lives was not lost on the informants. Some even ridiculed the idea of 'recruitment.' About ten percent of them questioned the very supposition that low participation in the profession had anything to do with recruitment. How can you recruit students who are not academically prepared? As one teacher said: 'Recruitment is not the answer. Preparation is the key.' (16/AFf) They claimed that the work must begin early on in the educational process, much, much earlier than most people presume, otherwise kids are lost. One teacher drew a poignant picture of the students that he works with on a daily basis:

> Kids are bored, disenchanted. They know that they're not going to college; they're misfits. We have little to offer them to keep their interest. As a result one-half are floating, one-fourth are being served, and one-fourth drop out. Kids are afraid to try, their minds are so scattered.
>
> (92/AFm)

Teachers contended that if students were better prepared in school, there would be a larger pool of students able to attend college and, hence, consider teaching as a career. One African American male expressed his concern at watching student failure continue over the years: 'Kids are lost by the way. They do not know how to transfer knowledge.' (37/AFm)

By focusing on the perceptions of school teachers, the research served as a form of intervention, providing teachers with the time and space for reflection on issues that were of major concern to them. Several times informants said that they had not previously seen the clear connection between their own actions in the classroom and how they might affect the future decision-making processes of their students. It was interesting to watch the changes in tenor as the interviews proceeded and a more sober tone gained prominence as teachers assessed their complicity in deflecting youthful aspirations from a career in teaching. Most came to the conclusion, as illustrated in the next comment, that if minority students had more positive experiences in school, they might be able to entertain the idea of a profession focused on educating others:

As children go through a school system, if they are successful, they may feel a desire to get involved as educators. The key is to get more minorities involved and successful in education, feeling that they are a part and that what they have to say is important to our system. There is a great need to build up self-esteem in Black students. Kids need to feel like they can succeed.

(17/AFm)

Recommendations to improve schooling had as much to do with the affective domain as the academic. Teachers did not see these as distinct but rather as intertwined and essential to quality teaching as illuminated in the statement: 'Students depend on caring; they need advising and counseling' (28/AFf). Specific suggestions included peer tutoring, support groups, language assistance for new immigrants, and vocational education for all children.

Related to enhancing kids' exposure to education was the awareness that students' lack of understanding of a system that they are subject to, but not in control of, could be the source of their resistance to it. Through more effective forms of bridging school life and home life, teachers could demonstrate the usefulness of classroom knowledge. An elderly Black male teacher whose father had taught until he was seventy years old reinforced this idea in proclaiming: 'Connect with what's happening in the community and jobs; take kids to the forest, to the hatchery. Show them how education works.' (94/AFm)

Another twist on this idea had to do with involvement with local businesses, not solely for the purpose of providing afterschool or summer employment but to expose students to the world of work and business. Maintaining that vibrant connection would help kids see how what they do today does, in fact, impact on their choices in the future. Two African American male teachers offered this advice: 'Get business into the schools and kids into businesses to see the real world. Students need strategies to see how to get there, to jobs and to a successful life' (96/AFm); 'Get business to step in as guests to supplement the teaching staff. They could adopt a school. K-3 [Kindergarten to Grade Three] really needs male models. Males too often go into administration; they're principals at an early age.' (17/AFm)

Improve the image of teachers

The importance of cultural and community influence cannot be overestimated. The myths and images created and maintained by a community about education seem to be one of the most powerful forces in determining whether their youth not only succeed in the educational enterprise but choose to engage in it as a career. The informants provided us with a host of recommendations as to how to increase positive involvement by the community in support of students of color entering teaching. One-fourth of them believed that if the image of teachers could be altered or improved, students of color might be more inclined to consider teaching as a career. The change in image would require a change in mindset on the part of American society that tends to denigrate teaching as if the profession was tangential rather than central to the advancement of the country. As one teacher reminded us: 'We must stop bashing teachers and show what good is being done.' (74/AFf)

But the damage done to the image of teachers is not only due to perceptions in the media and society; teachers themselves participate daily in the denigration of their own career. Negative attitudes about teaching, coming from the very people who have selected the profession, have the most powerful impact on students. As one Latino teacher claimed: 'Students do not identify with teachers nor are they empowered by them; this is not a class issue.' (72/LAm) To remedy the lack of awareness about the profession, another teacher encouraged teachers themselves to become better advocates for the profession:

> Acquaint them with the fact that being a teacher is a good thing. Teaching is a part of almost every profession. Identify the characteristics of a good teacher. See skills that they [students] have and link them with the teaching profession. Show that teachers do more than lecture. Take them to teachers' meetings. Most of what we do doesn't happen in classrooms. Get them into college prep courses. Have them work as a cohort group. Set up an evening or Saturday program for students to sit and talk about teaching.
>
> (46/AFf)

As intimated by the previous comment, most students know very little about what it takes to be a teacher or what a teacher really does. When teachers live in the community in which they teach, there is greater opportunity for them to take on a leadership role and for students and parents to see them as a resource for the community at large. During times of greater residential segregation many teachers who worked in inner cities lived in inner cities. This is not the case today. As professionals, teachers want the option to choose where and with whom they will practice their vocation. Part of the resistance to teaching in inner-city schools has to do with preconceptions of what teaching in this context is like. To counter these impressions some informants asserted the importance of promoting the positive characteristics of the profession: 'We need to turn the field around so as not to be so low status; market the good things' (89/ASm); 'We must get kids to see that being a teacher is helping.' (52/AFf)

Still others contended that the negative image of teachers could only be combated by taking a more professional stance. Professionalism as defined in the interviews did not have the same ring as that often heard in the teacher education literature (Darling-Hammond and Sclan, 1996). These informants equated professionalism with presentation of self and the field. A professional in their minds looked, behaved and spoke in a certain way as reflected in this comment: 'Have teachers professionally dressed who make presentations. Market professionalism.' (78/AFf) Better public relations had a home-grown feel to it. Although the media definitely affects young people's perception of the career options, these teachers knew that attitudes within the community were equally, if not more, powerful. In response to this they advocated: 'Have PR people go into the community. [Communicate the idea that] we care about your child, but we need you to help us. Talk it up. [Let them know that] there's something you get from teaching that money can't buy, giving back.' (66/AFf)

Encourage students

Twenty percent of the informants realized that students were not becoming teachers because no one was encouraging them to do so and wanted to see a major shift in the way youth are oriented to education and to the profession. This included increased exposure and mentoring, especially for African American children: 'There is a need to give Black children more experiential input at an early age. We need to augment their lack of experience from their families. We need to build up their self-esteem.' (17/AFm) One of the ways to institutionalize career awareness was to encourage kids to join organizations that gave them an introduction to what it might be like as a teacher. Informants believed that the earlier the better – waiting until high school, particularly for students of color, was much too late: 'Form FTA [Future Teachers of America] clubs. In the sixth grade kids need an idea of what they want to do' (21/AFf); 'We all have our calling; the key is to find what yours is as early as possible.' (85/AFm)

It is not unusual for people to assume that we need more teachers of color in order to ensure the success of minority youth. Although this is to some extent true, it can also be an excuse for non-minority status individuals to forsake kids of color and their responsibility to educate all children to the best of their ability. In conversations with these teachers, mentoring was seen as needed on all fronts by all concerned. Men, in particular, spoke passionately about this topic. Often, comments such as: 'Mentoring is important. Boys in general are being lost.' (37/AFm) came after a powerful story of how someone reached out to them and helped them turn a corner in their lives. Because of this, some of the teachers believed it their duty to give back what they had gained. An elderly male put it this way: 'It's my belief that you have to bring someone along.' (60/AFm) A Black female teacher trained in Latin and Greek who taught Classics at one of the poorest inner-city schools in her district summed it up in these words: 'We need mentors for kids; let them know that you are there. Get them hooked into teaching.' (41/AFf)

Involve parents

Throughout the interviews the importance of parental support continually resurfaced. Twenty percent of the informants noted that the involvement of parents is essential if we are to attract their children into the field of teaching. Even if parents are not formally educated, and perhaps particularly if they are not, they need to be included in the conversation. They need to be seen as part of guiding a student's overall education. As reflected in this comment from a Latina teacher, parents can and do have a powerful influence on career decisions:

> Start with parents in outreach. Parents keep kids home to help them [with household chores]. Parents need to know that their kids need an education. Give them the hard facts. Re-educate the parents. Bring them into the schools, and have schools go to them in the community. And you must give them all these things in their first languages. It's not that they don't care. They have an inferior feeling. Learn also from them.
>
> (7/LAf)

An African American teacher offered her view on Latino parental participation:

> We need to examine each culture and see how to reach them. For example, Hispanic parents don't like to come to school to harass the teachers, but they do go to church, so we need to go to church and work with them. Have a time to meet with parents and always serve food.
>
> (11/AFf))

Whether her view is valid for Latinos or not, such an explanation fit the perception of Native Americans by one Native teacher: 'Native American [parents] don't come to school; you need social functions to get them involved. Open the school to the community.' (109/NAm) Ideas to do this included providing hands-on computer training, parent rooms, math skill centers, cultural events, etc.

Many informants, however, perceived that parental attitudes towards school have changed. A large portion of the blame was placed on the fact that parents seemed younger and less experienced than in the past. The comment, 'kids raising kids,' echoed throughout the interview process and was apparently a major obstacle for teachers trying to solicit the help of parents in their children's education. Whether this is a perception that gains validity as one gets older or whether there is an element of truth, it was difficult to discern. But teachers were exasperated by the indifference they believed was coming from parents: 'Parents don't know how to support or respect. They think that the world is out to get them. Most parents are young. I contract with them that the child will do homework, but they don't' (70/AFf); 'We have parents who don't have morals and values. I want to tell them, "I care, you should care. I want you to feel free to come into my class anytime. You have to do your part, I'll do mine."' (87/AFm)

Related to the age of many urban parents was their lack of adequate education. These two factors usually corresponded with low income and a fear of the system. Parents did not want, or did not know how, to participate in the education of their children. Some of the comments from these teachers were clearly cries of desperation: 'My personal burnout is that parents don't respond.' (70/AFf)

> Getting the parents involved is one of my most difficult tasks. Often the parents are lacking knowledge on how to train kids. The average minority parent doesn't understand the impact that they have or could have on their children's education and success, such as limiting TV time. Education is a mystery to them, [they think] either you've got it or you don't.
>
> (17/AFm)

Two other female informants shared their fears and frustrations in attempting to access the parents of their students: 'Young parents put more responsibility on schools. It's difficult to get parents into school; they're not interested. I don't go to homes; I'm not sure how safe it is' (64/AFf); 'Parents can have a great influence. They get very irate and abuse teachers, in contrast to Asian children. It becomes a safety issue; we're attacked. We need to educate the parents.' (18/AFf) The extreme measures that a few teachers were willing to entertain can be seen in the following suggestion:

> You're going to have to reach the mothers as well as the kids. Maybe there should be a rule that you have to go to school to get welfare, or help out in the schools. Now welfare is too easy. You need to educate the parents, so they can teach the kids.
>
> (11/AFf)

Stress the importance of education

Stressing the value of education can lead to changes in priorities within the family and community as reflected in the next comments. One Black male teacher frustrated by his students' reluctance to be seen carrying books home said: 'Students need to see that they can be a success without feeling like a nerd.' (42/AFm) A colleague of the previous teacher further cajoled his students into high performance by alerting them to the fact college wasn't necessarily a given: 'I tell students – how are you going to get to college if you don't work (study) and get a scholarship?' (44/AFm) An Asian teacher explained her culture's attitude towards hard work, rather than ability, as a possible explanation for success in school, though as we saw in the previous chapter this did not transfer over into greater participation in teaching: 'We need to raise socially responsible children. In Japan, you are taught to persevere, above all. Endurance is heroic, in popular culture and in daily life.' (75/ASf)

Provide early teaching-like experiences and bring in role models

Almost one-third of the teachers believed that the most important factor in attracting more students of color to the field of teaching was providing hands-on classroom teaching experience early in their education. The problem seemed to be that there are far too few opportunities that allow this to occur. If students at all levels of K-12 could have the opportunity to tutor, advise or teach younger children in some capacity, they might become aware of their strengths in this area. If potential teachers could only get a taste of what it is like to turn a child's life around, informants contended, they would get hooked on teaching:

> Working with kids is what attracts people to the teaching field. It makes them realize that this is what they want to do. Any kind of teaching experiences would be helpful. Kids are not given the opportunity to see what it's like to teach. Targeting kids in high school who might be interested in teaching and then mentoring them would be a great idea.
>
> (12/AFf)

The concept of 'reaching back,' so common in communities of color, was further discussed specifically in terms of role models. Twenty percent of the informants claimed that such involvement on the part of the community was essential if we are to attract more students of color to the field of teaching. These role models were of two types: teachers of color and community people of color. The first need echoed most clearly in conversations with African American females who were raised in the South: 'More Black teachers need to be in the inner-city school; they're more familiar with the experience of kids. Males are especially needed.' (52/AFf) A male teacher angered by the district requirement that a school can only have so many minority teachers, commented: 'Get rid of the teacher racial balance. Fifty-fifty is better. Urban schools need more minority teachers.' (60/AFm) The way it was currently contrived in some schools with large minority populations is that there is a quota on how many minority teachers each school can have. Some teachers who want to teach in inner-city schools are assigned to the suburbs. In these cases the desire to spread teachers of color around the district did not serve them or the kids well.

Role models in the second instance involved people from the community who could provide positive life examples for minority youth. They did not have to be educators, but rather people who had succeeded because of their education. They could also be people who did not do well in school or who had not taken advantage of the educational opportunities they may have had at the time. These individuals could just as easily motivate young students into seeing education as an asset or how their life could have been made easier had they focused on education. One African American male teacher conceded: 'Black males are into the macho thing. Their role models are in sports. They could meet superstars who had a teacher as a role model.' (87/AFm) One Latino teacher was particularly excited by this idea:

> Bring older Hispanics to school, have them show how they can better themselves. Show them the negative sides, if they don't get an education. I believe in show and tell. Get them interested in the field. Bring college students into the classroom for one or two days.
>
> (4/LAm)

Recruit in the community

The lack of awareness on the part of students, especially potential first-generation college students, of what type of jobs are out there and what it takes to get those jobs is troubling. Almost twenty percent of the informants believed there is a growing need for community outreach and recruitment in a variety of forms. As one Latina suggested:

> Go out and talk to them; explain opportunities and the program. Explain that being bilingual gives them many opportunities in teaching. Explain that this nation will stay strong if all the students learn. Education is crucial. Explain that we need qualified people, sensitive to the students' needs. There are a lot of people who don't relate to students at a personal level in teaching.
>
> (9/LAf)

Several African American informants suggested: 'Go into the churches. I see kids in church working, identify these types. They can talk their language.' (51/AFf, 12/AFf) Similarly, a Latina shared an example of grass-roots outreach:

> A theatre group of three Hispanic guys came to our school. All were teachers, from very rough backgrounds. They had all got out of drugs.

They spoke the language of the kids and were more successful at reaching the kids than we ever could be.

(31/LAf)

For Native Americans, community outreach is an even more serious problem because of the negative experiences that many parents have had in boarding schools and the dislocation of many urban Indians. Because of this, ways are needed to develop trust and to connect them with their child's learning. One suggested: 'Go into the [Native American] community and make a commitment to the young.' (108/NAf)

In addition to calling for early intervention and establishing contacts in the community, a few teachers upbraided colleges for not looking in their own backyard, meaning that they should be contacting students of color already on college campuses about the advantages of being a teacher and then supporting their efforts to succeed. As one woman commented: 'Undecided college kids need to be picked up into teaching.' (43/AFf) This has been accomplished with success on a few campuses; one institution that is known for its positive work with Native American and Latina women was mentioned: 'At Heritage College the women couldn't leave the reservation to go to college, so the sisters (nuns) brought the college to them.' (77/NAf)

A Native American teacher reminds us that in addition to finding students on their own campuses, predominantly White colleges need to build bridges with other colleges that might be more successful attracting students of color. One informant explained the value in this approach: 'Have kids visit colleges and universities and see teachers in action, see the changes in the lives of students, especially at the Historically Black Colleges. They need to see secure people who know information and are imparting it to students.' (87/AFm) One young mixed-race male with an upper-class background, in referring to the demands of working with low-income kids, confessed: 'It seems like it almost has to come from upper-class Blacks, where they can afford [to do] something like this. You should go to the colleges and get them there.' (20/AFm).

Enhance financial aid options

According to ten percent of the informants, financial aid must increase if we are to attract more low-income students of color into the field of teaching. Such assistance can come in a variety of forms including scholarships, tuition breaks, loan forgiveness programs, part-time jobs on campus, and tutoring positions for pay. As explained by one informant: 'More opportunities for minorities would encourage more to go into teaching. Without hope of any support, minorities won't work as hard as necessary to go into teaching or into college.' (73/AFf) Although the rhetoric in many urban school districts claims a shortage of teachers, and particularly minority teachers, many of the interviews revealed financial hardships as one of the main reasons that students hesitate to go on to graduate school or a fifth-year program for their credential. One teacher lamented: 'The university has to say, "if you go into teacher education, we'll pay."' (59/AFm)

Others believed that job security was a factor in a student selecting teaching as a career, 'Guarantee them a job; security is important to minorities.' (46/AFf) This referred not to the tenure that teachers receive after three years of successful teaching but rather a job after receiving their credential. Some of the informants had spent several years as substitutes waiting for an opening. Few are the potential teachers who are able to survive this state of limbo. Students need to know the ropes of the profession and, if they make it through, they have to be able to move into a position that utilizes their talents. Confirming this view, one teacher said: 'If students knew earlier that they had a chance; and if they had the money, they would go into teaching.' (30/NAf)

Increase salary of teachers

About fifteen percent of the informants said at the onset that the best way to attract more minority youth into teaching was to simply raise the salary of teachers. There was little discussion on this point other than a few comments such as these: 'You need to offer incentives to get Black teachers to teach in the inner-city schools. They need more recognition.' (54/AFf) It is interesting that although this was often the first reason mentioned in the interviewing process as to why students were not entering the field of teaching, by the time we got to discussing how to encourage teaching careers, two-thirds of the way into a one- to two-hour interview, income had lost its significance. Far more important were the attitudes of the community, family, and teachers themselves towards the profession as filtered through their own experiences and expectations.

9 Interpretations

Professionalism and Community

Every modern culture requires schooling for full participation. When a culture requires something but blocks access to it, there is conflict. Schooling has long been the path to participation in modern life and thus inequalities of access to schooling have been contested on grounds of race, religion, region, gender, and class. We justify unequal results through the ideology of meritocracy but the reality is infused with the disadvantages of race and class (Pettigrew, 1974). Students in American urban classrooms do not have a choice – they must meet the requirements of modern life or be resigned to poverty, even though their families may represent a myriad of traditional cultures offering alternatives and lessons for modern life. The negotiation of a balance between the competing loyalties of traditional kinship and urban America takes place in schoolrooms and teachers need every multicultural insight available as they conduct that process. Teachers, however, are not simply instruments of modernization and professional expertise. Teachers have loyalties to identities and images from traditional cultures and local communities embodied in one or many generations of their kinfolk. The task of professional transformation must respect and address these loyalties in order to provide the optimum instruction for low-income, immigrant, and non-White students (Zeichner and Hoeft, 1996).

The theoretical context for my work extends Ogbu's cultural-ecological theory of school performance (Ogbu, 1995; Ogbu and Simons, 1998) to the role of community forces in the decision of students of color to become a teacher. I want to emphasize Ogbu's effort to strike a balance between structural factors, or 'the system,' and community forces, often expressed in a folk theory. As with Gibson (1991b) and others who have discussed Ogbu's work, I insist on the continuing importance of racism in any effort to understand the chronic underachievement of visible minority groups in the United States. Although we all too often conflate issues of race and class and neglect those of gender, American culture has remained a racialized situation in which the victims are forced to recognize their disadvantage while the White majority and less visible ethnic minorities can choose to ignore and misinterpret the effects of racism. That said, I find the work for this book most compelling in its portrayal of the community forces that reinforce the system in an effort to dissuade students of color from choosing to teach. I want to offer a brief conceptual framework in an effort to understand that process.

The focus of my framework is the role in the choice to teach of community images of teachers and the respect given to teachers by the adults of a community, including its teachers. I see the process as a result of four intersecting 'projects.' The concept of a project refers to the intentional creation of life's meaning as attempted by individuals acting in collaboration with others in similar circumstances and historical moments. The four projects relevant for our effort to understand the choice of a teaching career for students of color are those of *community, immigration, class*, and *profession*. The *community* project is the attempt to teach the young to take pride in their heritage, to return to the community in service, to know the history and ceremonies, and to continue traditional values that are embodied in the family and spiritual practices. The *immigrant* project is the effort to enter a new culture as a family, to gain advantages needed for survival through schooling and hard work, and to accept one's cultural identity, but not to worry about survival of culture in one's own hands. The *class* project focuses on the improvement of the individual's economic and social position through schooling, to build an improved position for one's immediate family within a given culture, and not to challenge that culture or to be concerned with the preservation of another culture. The *professional* project is an individual's attempt to attain certain occupational roles with high degrees of status and economic security, and to secure the benefits of such a position for one's family through education and cultural literacy, with the necessary diminishing of local loyalties. In the choice of teaching as a career on the part of young people within America's communities of color, these four projects intersect and compete within individual lives and identities. As teacher educators and citizens, we must seek to understand how each of the projects and their interaction relate to our efforts to find and prepare sufficient numbers of competent and culturally relevant teachers for our urban schools.

Teaching in 'traditional' communities gains respect as a crucial support for the dignity of that community. There is little mobility through immigration or economic means and the passing on of cultural heritage is a stable, honored profession that rests securely within the *community* project. When mobility of place or class enters the lives of a whole cultural group, that group encounters schooling as an outside agent, both as a means to necessary acculturation but also as opposition or even the destroyer of dignity resting in the traditional culture of the immigrant or upwardly mobile group. Schooling is the principal means for individuals to escape the local context through career mobility, the *professional* project, as defined by the larger, dominant culture while also the principal threat to the continuity of cultural identities. The *immigrant* project accepts such tension as the price of its success and its heroes are defined by winning a place in the new culture while paying respect to their immigrant roots. Such a tension is much more troubling within a *community* project that seeks sustenance for local institutions, families, and ways of life.

Within both the *immigrant* and *class* projects, the teaching career is an available avenue to success that can be shared with family although not as clearly with the larger community. The necessary adoption of the *professional* project by successful individuals is taken for granted as a mark of that success. For the *community* project, professional identity is much more problematic. Professional life has its own demands for loyalties and lifestyles that compete or even overshadow loyalties to traditional community, family, and spiritual practices. As a cultural group experiences the loss of its youth to the *professional* project, the institutions responsible represent a threat to the very existence of a traditional community. The crucial institution for professional life in modern culture is the school. All candidates for the opportunities that advance the life chances of immigrant and working-class families must meet the competitive challenges of schooling for at least sixteen years of their youth. Strength for that process comes from a strong cultural base, a knowledge of ceremony, sufficient economic stability, and a supportive family. Even White working-class kids are handicapped if they are confused about their cultural identity – a steady job, religious activity, and family support all contribute to success in an otherwise unremarkable child. For children of non-White, immigrant, urban, and rural families of working-class families, the prospects are few even if those supports are present. What often complicates the process goes by many names but can be approached as the intense conflict among the four projects suggested here. Children of non-White identities in America's cities face the demands of professionalism with few supports and with the additional burden of risking the cultural identity that has sustained their families and communities through generations of oppression and discrimination while enduring lives of labor.

Image and Respect: The Choice to Teach

Teaching as a profession lacks color. Teachers, as professionals and regardless of their race, gender, class, or any cultural identity, allegedly possess a general or universal expertise that can be applied to any student within the well-managed world of the school building. To suggest that teaching might have color and that racial or other identities could be relevant in the recruitment and effectiveness of teachers is to call into question the very definition of a profession. In the world of urban school teaching in the United States, race and racism are endemic. Schooling is conducted within a social context that embodies racial assumptions and practices on an everyday basis and that rests on a history of racism. If we are to understand the 'color of teaching,' we must come to terms with the role of racial identity in the selection, recruitment, and retention of the teachers desperately needed for the students of urban America in all of their cultural diversity, economic deprivation, and subjugation to the racial myths ingrained in American life. Racial identity in the United States combines pride of heritage and a consciousness of oppression, both past and on-going, imposed on non-White individuals who often face the additional burdens of immigration and poverty. When we ask youth of color to assume the tasks of preparing to teach, we must acknowledge the difficult negotiation between their racial identity with its legacy of racial striving and their personal goals of an exemplary education. The successful resolution of that negotiation may mean the undoing of a modern consensus on the nature of professional teacher education. The canons of learning theory, standardized curricula and testing, hierarchical administration, graded classes, and agreements about how a teacher looks and performs may all be called into question as we strive for a more inclusive schooling in American society (Gordon, 1998).

The preparation needed for teachers of urban students challenges the generic professionalism of teacher education as we have known it for nearly 200 years. If urban schools have realities that are unrecognized in the orthodoxies of teacher education, we face a complex task of identifying the personal qualities and the professional preparation needed in the teachers we assign to those schools (Haberman, 1996; Foster, 1995). A history of segregation in American schooling provides a troubling backdrop for that challenge. Within White culture, exceptional individuals are allowed to bridge the borders of class and religion without representing any group and thus demonstrate the meritocratic fairness of the system. The process has extended to non-White individuals who can either pass as 'White' or who demonstrate extraordinary adaptability to norms of White culture as applied to non-White individuals (Matute-Bianchi, 1991). However, when group improvement and intergroup competition enter the process as in affirmative action or other compensatory measures, the individual person of color must accept both the benefits and costs of visible minority status. The choices include an acceptance of the privileges of exceptionalism, thus the attraction of a 'luck' notion of success, or an insistence on 'communal' uplift in the form of political movements or community work. The communal option tends to minimize the professionalization of the individual by creating a distance from the obvious norms of White culture. A communal approach also softens the professional requirements of a career, including scholarship for its own sake, in a highly competitive and individualist context for which first-generation professionals may not be prepared. That preparation requires early and continuous identification with school work and its most obvious practitioners – teachers.

For students of color, acquisition of a quality school education is crucial. Those students who are succeeding in school then need to be motivated to choose teaching as a career. One obvious, but seldom acknowledged, source of motivation comes daily from their school teachers. Unfortunately, what teachers say about their profession is seldom positive. The power of a teacher's attitude towards career decision making is not lost on young people, especially if they are working-class students with few educated professionals in their lives. A second potential source of positive image-making comes from attitudes about the teaching profession that are shared with students by their family and community adults. Students are motivated to succeed in school if they understand the results of their effort to be in line with their personal goals. If they receive support and encouragement to stay in school and achieve goals that are relevant to schooling, then they will consider the professions that follow from successful schooling. If one of those professions is school teaching, then that becomes one of the motivating goals for high performance in school. The cycle continues as that performance opens up the choice of teaching as a career.

In the process of conducting interviews with veteran teachers and influential adults within communities of color, a pattern emerged that caused me to pause. Rather than today's youth not listening to or respecting elders, as is the common belief, they are in fact acting on the expectations and aspirations of the adults within their communities. The main expectation for youth of color who are college-educated is that they would take high-paying jobs that would bring status to the family – they would not go into teaching or become involved in community-oriented work. Ironically, these same young people were criticized for being materialistic and lacking the self-sacrifice required of someone entering teaching. In contrast to these adult perceptions, I have found in my interviews with college students of color a strong desire to return to their communities to assist in providing a ladder for the next generation. Because most of these students have been discouraged from realizing this goal in the form of a career in teaching, they resort to majoring in related but more amorphous fields such as Community Studies, American Studies, Sociology, Ethnic Studies, or Women's Studies. It is as if the admission of interest in teaching as a profession shows a failure to use their higher education to the utmost advantage. Many students I know have taken numerous courses in education and intend to go into teaching but still have not been able to tell their parents for fear of ridicule.

My contention is that students of color are not shying away from entering the teaching profession. They know, better than anyone, how important a significant adult can be in their lives. They have just emerged from a system where they survived because at least one teacher was there to guide them. The impediments they face when considering a career in teaching center on the attitudes that surround them, that affect them, and that humiliate them as future teachers. The image of teaching as a 'namby-pamby,' 'goody-two-shoes,' part-time, female job with 'summers off with the kids' still lingers even as the actual requirements for the profession demand highly competent, computer-skilled, multilingual, dynamic individuals who can handle kids from every walk of life. Many United States schools are in session year-round; violence in schools is increasing; a grasp of global politics and international economies is essential for understanding local job options and aspirations. Still, we refuse to relinquish our images of teachers and their importance.

The form that professionalism takes on the part of teachers is critical in the negotiation facing potential teachers of color. If teacher professionalism moves toward individual advancement and professional 'community' with resultant distance from students and families, lack of concern with dress and appearance, and a casual attitude toward student outcomes, then students of color, especially of the working class, are unlikely to see themselves in that role; and parents of these students will discourage teaching as a profession. If professionalism is directed toward service for youth, student outcomes, and presentation of a professional self in school, then young people will be more likely to aspire to that role and be able to develop a concept of professionalism that contributes to their welfare and to the welfare of their family and community. Both the image presented by teachers and the respect given teachers by a community rest within the ways the majority culture and minority cultures interact with a professional culture. Within both the non-American home cultures and/or the minority communities, teachers are both more respected and present a more elite image than within the American majority culture. When minority teachers attempt to present themselves accordingly, they are resisted both by the lack of respect from the majority culture and by the less elite image adopted by most teaching professionals from the majority culture. Teachers of color, including newer immigrants, are expected to adopt the norms of the majority culture and its teaching profession while also attempting to meet the expectations for their elite position within communities of color. The problem of lack of respect and negative image, therefore, seems to lie less with communities of color and more with the dominant society. Integrating into mainstream America means adapting to different attitudes and values, ones that focus on acquisition and individualism. As each group becomes more aware of the low status of teaching within mainstream, adopted culture, they begin to take on those same attitudes. The assumption expressed by the teachers interviewed held that in order to survive in this 'society' you acquire the dominant stance, which in this case was to see teachers as less valuable than entrepreneurs. This process has assisted in the denigration of the teaching profession in the eyes of many teachers of color.

The dominant White liberal view claims that we should be respected for our capabilities, not for the way we present ourselves. However, professional people of color are aware that, first, it is important to differentiate themselves within their own people based on class in order to demonstrate not only their personal success, but also a respect for the profession of teaching as traditionally held within ethnic minority cultures. Second, once they leave the protected space of their job and school they are on their own as representatives of their race. The dominant culture will often treat them based on how they look. Third, they must provide an example for children of their own community as role models and for children of other cultures in order to break down stereotypes and develop a positive image of teaching by a person of color.

From this work we can consider the notion that the negative values that have been attributed to 'newcomers' into mainstream society might in fact be 'American values.' Immigrants, migrants, and visible ethnic minorities, in their attempt to emulate mainstream society, reflect back that which is most painfully disabling about American society. Dominant values in a 'free-market society' are not community-oriented, do not respect service-oriented professions, and do not support assistance to those most in need. Unfamiliar with the nuances that mask the brutality of the 'rugged individual,' many 'minority peoples' act out that which mainstream America has the most difficult time dealing with: its own greed. As demands for greater assimilation increase, we must be aware of the repercussions. If mainstream America refuses to respect teachers, how can we expect 'minority' cultures, who are asked to emulate and assimilate into the dominant culture's values, to respect teachers.

Changes are required at a fundamental level, including the acknowledgement that teaching is not only valuable but essential to the future of any society. Teaching is one of the most difficult and complex professions. Although the salaries are not high, they are commensurate with many other professions in which the clientele is not pre-selected for ability to pay. Families and communities must realize that their strength is directly linked to the quality of education that their children receive. The most effective way to guide that change is to be a part of it in terms of actual participation in the teaching force. In my overall work, I am interested in issues of meaning-making and how the meaning of one's work is affected by ethnic and socioeconomic status as well as regionalism, education, and immigration. If we are to have sufficient able teachers for America's urban schools, students of color must find that meaning in their choice to be a teacher – and the guidance of their communities and their teachers must show the way.

A Note on Sources

My work for this book rests on a broad and varied foundation of others' research and writing. I want to briefly mention the work that was most influential in my own preparation. The cited works are only tokens of authors' works that suggest the nature of their influence. My work on teachers and teacher education was launched by John Goodlad (1984, 1990a, 1990b) and his far-reaching program of research and commentary. My approach to interviewing and ethnographic research was aided though not defined by the guidance of Howard Becker (1998) and Mishler's framework (1986). Stanfield (1994) helped to clarify the racialized nature of social science research and set a demanding standard for work such as mine.

As I pursued the issues of ethnic diversity in teacher education programs and in the recruitment of new teachers, I was guided by insights from Willie (1978), Lawrence-Lightfoot (1983, 1994), Hilliard (1988), Haberman (1987,1996), Cardenas and Cardenas (1977) and Comer (1988). Collectively, their guidance helped me hone my insights into the complexity of issues facing students of color in urban communities. The work of James Banks (1991), Grant (1988) and Butler and Walter (1991) provided the conceptual frameworks for approaching multicultural education and the role of ethnic studies in teacher education.

My primary theoretical debt is to Professor John Ogbu (1974, 1988, 1991, 1995, 1998) whose work on the achievement of minority students as a function of their immigrant status pointed me to the role of community forces in the choice to become a teacher. Work closely related to Ogbu's that has been especially influential includes that of Fordham (1986, 1996), Gibson (1988, 1991b), and De Vos (1980).

Michael Knapp's work (Knapp and Shields, 1990) on the importance of poverty and social class structure in urban schooling reinforced my own priority for including a class analysis in any understanding of minority student achievement and diversity among teachers. My general understanding of class issues had one foot planted in the work of Bernstein (1973, 1996), Bourdieu and Passeron (1977), Bowles and Gintis (1976) and Willis (1977) and the other in my own experience of working-class life that echoed the voices captured in the work of Shor (1980). Rist (1970) and Metz (1990) added an important challenge to my thinking on the role of socioeconomic class in the school context of teaching.

The effort to understand the role of race in American schooling is a never-ending one. William M. Banks (1996) provided a helpful perspective while the work of Omi and Winant (1986) offered the guiding framework. Smedley (1993) and Forbes (1990) helped put the construction of racial categories in a fuller context. Claude Steele (1992) contributed a crucial insight on racial identity and schooling that still needs to find its adequate expression in my work. Kozol (1991) has been a 'fire in the belly' throughout my study of urban schools. The work of the Spindlers (1987, 1990) and their many collaborators has been invaluable in my reaching a broader under-standing of how cultural forces outside of school must be addressed in any study of schooling. Heath and McLaughlin (1993) pointed out clearly the intersection of class and race in school achievement. Orfield's (1994) work reminds us of the ever present reality of continued racial segregation. The insights of Seymour Sarason (1993a, b) have guided my work toward a more ecological framework while Waller's (1932) classic text is still an inspiration for honest and deliberate investigation of the social role of the classroom teacher.

My work necessitated at least a preliminary study of the history of the teaching profession in the United States. The general outline was provided by Warren's (1989) anthology as well as the work of Tyack (1987) and Herbst (1989a, b). Of special value in Warren (1989) were the contributions of Johnson (1989), Rury (1989), and Carter (1989). The history of African American teaching is now a flourishing field and with Anderson's work (1988) as a foundation, I took full advantage of the rich offerings by Perkins (1989), Foster (1995, 1997), Delpit (1995), Joyce King (1994), Dilworth (1988), Sabrina King (1993), and Ladson-Billings (1994).

The study of Latino history and culture has been a rewarding effort and a few of the authors who have been especially helpful are the Suarez-Orozcos (1989, 1998), Trueba (1989) and Shorris (1992). Rumbaut (1995) provided the needed basic work on the schooling needs of immigrant children. My work toward understanding Native American perspectives received crucial guidance from the writings of Deloria (1988), Adams (1988), Allen (1986), and Reyhner (1991) as well as the fine review article of Lomawaima (1995). Unger's (1977) small book on the child welfare disaster of Native American life was a special inspiration. Tierney's (1992) work helped me grasp the complexities of higher education for Native American youth. Spring (1994), in his consistently challenging way, brought home the cultural tension of the Native American student. My grasp of how Asian cultures have impacted on schooling in the United States rests on my own study of East Asian languages and culture as well as on work in Japan and Taiwan. Takaki (1989) provided the needed overview of Asian American history while

Kitano and Daniels (1988), Nakanishi and Nishida (1995), and Goodwin and Genishi (Goodwin et al., 1997) all guided my work in the experience of schooling and school teaching for Asian Americans.

This note is not meant to be a comprehensive survey of relevant work; for such a survey one would start with the handbooks edited by Banks and Banks (1995), Sikula (1996) and Denzin and Lincoln (1994). Of special value for my work were the articles in the *Handbook of Research in Teacher Education* by Darling-Hammond and Sclan (1996), Schwartz (1996), Zeichner and Hoeft (1996) and Boyer and Baptiste (1996). Articles by Knapp and Woolverton (1995), and Lee and Slaughter-Defoe (1995) in the *Handbook on Research on Multicultural Education* offered crucial contributions to my work.

References

AACTE (1994) 'Teacher education pipeline III: Schools, colleges, and departments of education enrollments by race, ethnicity, and gender', Washington, DC: American Association of Colleges for Teacher Education, ED 369 780.

Abalos, D. T. (1986) *Latinos in the United States: The Sacred and the Political*, South Bend, IN: University of Notre Dame Press.

Adair, A. V. (1984) *Desegregation: The Illusion of Black Progress*, New York: University Press of America.

Adams, D. W. (1988) 'Fundamental considerations: The deep meaning of Native American schooling, 1880–1900', *Harvard Educational Review*, **58** 1, pp. 1–28.

Aguirre, A. Jr and Martinez, R. O. (1994) 'Chicanos in Higher Education: Issues and Dilemmas for the 21st Century', *ERIC Clearinghouse on Higher Education*, **ED36506**, pp. 1–3.

Allen, P. G. (1986) *The Sacred Hoop: Recovering the Feminine in American Indian Tradition*, Boston, MA: Beacon Press.

Anderson, J. D. (1988) *The Education of Blacks in the South, 1860–1935*, Chapel Hill, NC : The University of North Carolina Press.

Apple, M. W. (1986) *Teachers and Texts: A Political Economy of Class and Gender Relations in Education*, New York: Routledge.

Aronowitz, S. (1992) *The Politics of Identity: Class, Culture, Social Movements*, London: Routledge.

Aronowitz, S. and Giroux, H. A. (1991) 'Class, race and gender in educational politics', in Aronowitz, S. and Giroux, H. A., (Eds.), *Postmodern Education: Politics, Culture and Social Criticism*, Minneapolis, MN: University of Minnesota Press, pp. 3–55.

Asante, M. K. (1991) 'The afrocentric idea in education', *Journal of Negro Education*, **60**, 2, pp. 170–180.

Auerbach, E. R. (1995) 'The politics of the ESL classroom: Issues of power in pedagogical choices', in Tollefson, J. W., (Ed.), *Power and Inequality in Language Education*, Cambridge: Cambridge University Press, pp. 9–33.

Banks, J. A. (1991) *Teaching Strategies for Ethnic Studies*, Boston, MA: Allyn and Bacon.

Banks, J. A. and Banks, C. A. M. (1989) *Multicultural Education: Issues and Perspectives*, Boston, MA: Allyn and Bacon.

Banks, J. A. and Banks, C. A. M. (1995) (Eds.), *Handbook on Research on Multicultural Education*, New York: Macmillan

Banks, W. M. (1996) *Black Intellectuals: Race and Responsibility in American Life*, New York: W. W. Norton & Company.

Baruth, L. G. and Manning, M. L. (1992) *Multicultural Education of Children and Adolescents*, Needham Heights, MA: Allyn and Bacon.

Becker, H. S. (1998) *Tricks of the Trade: How to Think About Your Research While You're Doing It*, Chicago, IL: University of Chicago Press.

Bernstein, B. (1973) *Class, Codes, and Control*, St Albans: Paladin.

Bernstein, B. (1996) *Pedagogy, Symbolic Control and Identity*, London: Taylor and Francis.

Birmingham, S. (1977) *Certain People: America's Black Elite*, Boston, MA: Little, Brown and Co.

Book, C., Byers, J., and Freeman, D. H. (1983) 'Student expectations and teacher education traditions with which we can and cannot live', *Journal of Teacher Education*, **34**, pp. 9–13.

Bourdieu, P. and Passeron, J. (1977) *Reproduction in Education, Society and Culture*, London: Sage Publications.

Bowles, S. and Gintis, H. (1976) *Schooling in Capitalist America*, New York: Basic Books.

Boyer, J. B. and Baptiste, H. P. Jr (1996) 'The crisis in teacher education in America: Issues of recruitment and retention of culturally different (minority) teachers', in Sikula, J., (Ed.), *Handbook of Research in Teacher Education*, Second Edition, New York: Macmillan, pp. 779–794.

Butler, J. E. and Walter, J. C. (1991) (Eds.), *Transforming the Curriculum: Ethnic Studies and Women's Studies*, Albany, NY: State University of New York Press.

Cardenas, J. A. and Cardenas, B. (1977) *Theory of Incompatibilities, a Conceptual Framework for Responding to the Educational Needs of Mexican American Children*, San Antonio, TX: Intercultural Development Research Association.

Carnegie Forum on Education and the Economy (1986) *A Nation Prepared: Teachers for the 21st Century*, New York: Carnegie.

Carter, S. B. (1989) 'Incentives and rewards to teaching', in Warren, D., (Ed.), *American Teachers: Histories of a Profession at Work*, New York: Macmillan, pp. 49–64.

Chinoy, E. (1955) *Automobile Workers and the American Dream*, New York: Doubleday.

Clifford, G. J. (1989) 'Man/woman/teacher: Gender, family, and career in American educational history', in Warren, D., (Ed.), *American Teachers: Histories of a Profession at Work*, New York: Macmillan, pp. 293–344.

Cole, B. P. (1986) 'The black educator: An endangered species', *Journal of Negro Education*, **55**, 3, pp. 326–334.

Comer, J. P. (1988) 'Educating poor minority children', *Scientific American*, **259**, November, pp. 42–48.

Contreras, R. A. and Valverde, L. A. (1994) 'The impact of Brown on the education of Latinos', *Journal of Negro Education*, **63**, 3, pp. 170–81.

Cummins, J. (1986) 'Empowering minority students: A framework for intervention', *Harvard Educational Review*, **56**, 1, pp. 18–36.

Darling-Hammond, L. and Sclan, E. M. (1996) 'Who teaches and why: Dilemmas of building a profession for twenty-first century schools', in Sikula, J., (Ed.), *Hand-*

book of Research in Teacher Education, Second Edition, New York: Macmillan, pp. 67–101.

De Hoyos, A. (1961) 'Occupational and educational levels of aspiration of Mexican-American youth', *Dissertation Abstracts International*, 22/05, 61–02687, East Lansing, MI: Michigan State University.

De La Vega, M. (1951) 'Some factors affecting leadership of Mexican Americans in high school', unpublished dissertation, Los Angeles, CA: University of Southern California.

De Vos, G. A. (1980) 'Ethnic adaptation and minority status', *Journal of Cross-Cultural Psychology*, **11**, 1, pp. 101–124.

Deloria, V. (1988) *Custer Died for Your Sins*, Norman, OK: University of Oklahoma Press.

Delpit, L. D. (1988) 'The silenced dialogue: Power and pedagogy in educating other people's children', *Harvard Educational Review*, **58**, 3, pp. 280–298.

Delpit, L. D. (1995) *Other People's Children: White Teachers, Students of Color, and Other Cultural Conflicts in the Classroom*, New York: New Press.

Dentzer, Emily and Wheelock, Anne (1990) *Locked in/locked out: Tracking in Boston Public Schools*, Boston, MA: Massachusetts Advocacy Center.

Denzin, N. K. and Lincoln, Y. S. (1994) (Eds.), *Handbook of Qualitative Research*, Thousand Oaks, CA: Sage Publications.

Deyhle, D. (1992) 'Constructing failure and maintaining cultural identity: Navajo and Ute school leavers', *Journal of American Indian Education*, **31**, 2, pp. 24–47.

Dilworth, M. E. (1988) 'Black teachers: A vanishing tradition', *The Urban League Review*, **11**, 1, 2, pp. 54–58.

Dilworth, M. E. (1992) (Ed.), *Diversity in Teacher Education: New Expectations*, San Francisco, CA: Jossey-Bass

Domino, G. and Hannah, M. T. (1987) 'A comparative analysis of social values of Chinese and American children', *Journal of Cross-Cultural Psychology*, **18**, 1, pp. 58–77.

Doston, G. A. and Bolden, S. H. (1991) 'The impact of nationwide school reform on the recruitment and retention of black males in teacher education: A philosophical perspective', a paper presented at Fifth Annual Conference on Recruitment and Retention of Minorities in Education, Lexington, KY.

Dougherty, J. (1998) '"That's when we were marching for jobs": Black teachers and the early civil rights movement in Milwaukee', *History of Education Quarterly*, **38**, 2, pp. 121–141.

Dupre, B. B. (1986) 'Problems regarding the survival of future Black teachers in education', *Journal of Negro Education*, **55**, pp. 56–66.

Duran, R. P. (1983) *Hispanics' Education and Background: Predictors of College Achievement*, New York: College Entrance Examination Board.

Fairclough, N. (1992) *Critical Language Awareness*, London: Longman.

Fernandez, R. and Guskin, J. (1981) 'Hispanic students and school desegregation', in Hawley, W. D., (Ed.), *Effective School Desegregation: Equity, Quality, and Feasibility*, London: Sage Publications.

Forbes, J. D. (1990) 'The manipulation of race, caste, and identity: Classifying Afroamericans, Native Americans and Red-black people', *Journal of Ethnic Studies*, **17**, 4, pp. 1–51.

Fordham, S. (1996) *Blacked Out: Dilemmas of Race, Identity and Success at Capital High*, Chicago, IL: University of Chicago.

Fordham, S. and Ogbu, J. U. U. (1986) 'Black students' success: Coping with the burden of "acting white."' *The Urban Review*, **18**, pp. 176–206.

Foster, M. (1994) 'Effective black teachers: A literature review', in Hollins, E. R., King, I. E., and Hayman, W. C., (Eds.), *Teaching Diverse Populations: Formulating a Knowledge Base*, Albany, NY: State University of New York Press, pp. 225–242.

Foster, M. (1995) 'African American teachers and culturally relevant pedagogy', in Banks, J. A. and Banks, C. A. M., (Eds.), *Handbook on Research on Multicultural Education*, New York: Macmillan, pp. 570–81.

Foster, M. (1997) *Black Teachers on Teaching*, New York: New Press.

Fukurai, H. and Davies, D. (1998) 'Races people play: social de-construction of race, racial identity, statutory passing, and views on resource allocations and legal protections', Paper presented at American Sociological Association, San Francisco, CA.

Gaines, K. K. (1996). *Uplifting the Race: Black Leadership, Politics, and Culture in the Twentieth Century*, Chapel Hill, NC: University of North Carolina.

Gandara, P. (1995) *Over the Ivy Walls: The Educational Mobility of Low-Income Chicanos*, Berkeley, CA: California Policy Seminar.

Garcia, E. E. (1995) 'Educating Mexican American students: Past treatment and recent developments in theory, research, policy, and practice', in Banks, J. A. and Banks, C. A. M., (Eds.), *Handbook on Research on Multicultural Education*, New York: Macmillan, pp. 372–387.

Garcia-Castanon, J. (1994) 'Training Hmong refugee students', in Spindler, G. D. and Spindler, L., (Eds.), *Pathways to Cultural Awareness*, Thousand Oaks, CA: Corwin Press, pp. 197–219.

Gay, G. (1990) 'Achieving educational equality through curriculum desegregation', *Phi Delta Kappan*, **72**, September, pp. 56–62.

Gibson, M. A. (1988) *Accommodation Without Assimilation: Sikh Immigrants in an American High School*, New York: Cornell University Press.

Gibson, M. A. (1991a) 'Ethnicity, gender and social class: The school adaptation patterns of West Indian youths', in Gibson, M. A. and Ogbu, J. U. U., (Eds.), *Minority Status and Schooling: A Comparative Study of Immigrant and Involuntary Minorities*, New York: Garland Publishing, pp. 169–203.

Gibson, M. A. (1991b) 'Minorities and schooling: Some implications', in Gibson, M. A. and Ogbu, J. U. U., (Eds.), *Minority Status and Schooling: A Comparative Study of Immigrant and Involuntary Minorities*, New York: Garland Publishing, pp. 357–381.

Gibson, M. A. and Ogbu, J. U. U. (1991) (Eds.), *Minority Status and Schooling: A Comparative Study of Immigrant and Involuntary Minorities*, New York: Garland Publishing.

Gifford, B. R. (1986) 'Excellence and equity in teacher competency testing: A policy perspective', *Journal of Negro Education*, **55**, 3, pp. 251–271.

Giroux, H. A. (1994) 'Doing cultural studies: Youth and the challenge of pedagogy', *Harvard Educational Review*, **64**, 3, pp. 278–308.

References

Gomez, M. L. (1993) 'Prospective teachers' perspectives on teaching diverse children: a review with implications for teacher education and practice', *Journal of Negro Education*, **62**, 4, pp. 459–474.

Gonzales, G. G. (1990) *Chicano Education in the Era of Segregation*, Philadelphia, PA: Balch Institute.

Goodlad, J. I. (1984) *A Place Called School*, New York: McGraw-Hill.

Goodlad, J. I. (1990) *Teachers for Our Nation's Schools*, San Francisco, CA: Jossey-Bass.

Goodlad, J. I., Soder, R., and Sirotnik, K. A. (1990) *Places Where Teachers Are Taught*, San Francisco: Jossey-Bass.

Goodman, R. (1990) *Japan's 'International Youth': The Emergence of a New Class of Schoolchildren*, Oxford: Clarendon Press.

Goodwin, A. L., Genishi, C., Asher, N., and Woo, K. A. (1997) 'Voices from the margins: Asian American teachers' experiences in the profession', in Byrd, D. M. and McIntyre, D. J., (Eds.), *Teacher Education Yearbook V*, Thousand Oaks, CA: Association of Teacher Educators and Corwin Press.

Gordon, J. A. (1997a) 'A critical interpretation of policies for minority culture college students', *NACADA Journal*, **17**, 1, pp. 15–21.

Gordon, J. A. (1997b) 'Teachers of color speak to issues of respect and image', *The Urban Review*, **29**, 1, pp. 41–66.

Gordon, J. A. (1998) 'Caring through control: Reaching urban African American youth', *Journal of Just and Caring Education*, **4**, 4, pp. 418–440.

Gougeon, T. D. (1993) 'Urban schools and immigrant families: Teacher perspectives', *The Urban Review*, **25**, 4, pp. 251–287.

Grant, C. A. (1988) 'The persistent significance of race in schooling', *Elementary School Journal*, **88**, 5, pp. 561–69.

Grant, C. A. and Secada, W. G. (1989) 'Preparing teachers for diversity', in Houston, W. R., Haberman, M., and Sikula, J., (Eds.), *Handbook of Research on Teacher Education*, New York: Macmillan, p. 269.

Grant, C. A. and Sleeter, C. E. (1989) *Turning on Learning: Five Approaches for Multicultural Teaching Plans for Race, Class, Gender, and Disability*, Columbus, OH: Merrill.

Haberman, M. (1987) *Recruiting and Selecting Teachers for Urban Schools*, New York: ERIC/CUE.

Haberman, M. (1996) 'Selecting and preparing culturally competent teachers for urban schools', in Sikula, J., (Ed.), *Handbook of Research in Teacher Education*, Second Edition, New York: Macmillan, pp. 747–760.

Hale-Benson, J. E. (1982) *Black Children: Their Roots, Culture, and Learning Styles*, Baltimore, MD/London: John Hopkins University Press.

Harmon, A. (1990). 'When is an Indian not an Indian? "Friends of the Indian" and the problems of Indian identity', *Journal of Ethnic Studies*, 18(2), 95–123.

Hartman, J. S. and Askounia, A. C. (1989) 'Asian American students: Are they really a "model minority"?', *School Counselor*, **37**, 2, pp. 85–88.

Haycock, K. and Duany, L. (1991) 'Developing the potential of Latino students', *Principal*, **70**, 3, pp. 25–27.

Heath, S. B. and McLaughlin, M. W. (1993) 'Casting the self: Frames for identity and dilemmas for policy', in Heath, S. B. and McLaughlin, M. W., (Eds.), *Identity and Inner-City Youth: Beyond Ethnicity and Gender*, New York: Teachers College Press, pp. 210–238.

Herbst, J. (1989a) *And Sadly Teach*, Madison, WI: University of Wisconsin Press.

Herbst, J. (1989b) 'Teacher preparation in the nineteenth century: Institutions and purposes', in Warren, D., (Ed.), *American Teachers : Histories of a Profession at Work*, New York: Macmillan, pp. 213–256.

Hilliard, A. G. I. (1988) 'Reintegration for education: Black community involvement with black schools', *Urban League Review*, **11**, 1,2, pp. 201–208.

Holmes Group (1986) *Tomorrow's Teachers: A Report of the Holmes Group*, East Lansing, MI: The Holmes Group.

Horton, J. O. and Horton, L. E. (1979) *Black Bostonians: Family Life and Community Struggle in the Antebellum North*, New York: Holmes and Meier.

Irvine, J. J. (1988) 'An analysis of the problem of disappearing black educators', *Elementary School Journal*, **88**, pp. 503–513.

Johnson, W. R. (1989) 'Teachers and teacher training in the twentieth century', in Warren, D., (Ed.), *American Teachers : Histories of a Profession at Work*, New York: Macmillan, pp. 237–256.

Kao, G. and Tienda, M. (1995) 'Optimism and achievement: The educational performance of immigrant youth', *Social Science Quarterly*, **76**, 1, pp. 1–19.

Keefe, S. E. and Padilla, A. M. (1987) *Chicano Ethnicity*, Albuquerque, NM: University of New Mexico Press.

King, J. E. (1994) 'The purpose of schooling for African American children: Including cultural knowledge', in Hollins, E. R., King, J. E., and Hayman, W. C., (Eds.), *Teaching Diverse Populations: Formulating a Knowledge Base*, Albany, NY: State University of New York Press, pp. 25–44.

King, J. E. and Ladson-Billings, G. (1990) 'The teacher education challenge in elite university settings: Developing critical perspectives for teaching in a democratic and multicultural society', *European Journal of Intercultural Studies*, **1**, 2, pp. 15–30.

King, S. H. (1993) 'The Limited Presence of African-American Teachers', *Review of Educational Research*, **63**, 2, pp. 115–150.

Kitano, H. and Daniels, R. (1988) *Asian Americans: Emerging Minorities*, Englewood Cliffs, NJ: Prentice-Hall.

Kluckhohn, C. (1962) *Culture and Behavior*, New York: The Free Press of Glencoe.

Knapp, M. S. and Shields, P. M. (1990) *Better Schooling for the Children of Poverty: Alternatives to Conventional Wisdom*, Washington, DC: US Government Printing Office.

Knapp, M. S. and Woolverton, S. (1995) 'Social Class and Schooling', in Banks, J. A. and Banks, C. A. M., (Eds.), *Handbook of Research on Multicultural Education*, New York: Macmillan, pp. 548–569.

Kozol, J. (1991) *Savage Inequalities*, New York: Crown.

Kramer, B. J. (1991) 'Education and American Indians: The experience of the Ute Indian Tribe', in Gibson, M. A. and Ogbu, J. U. U., (Eds.), *Minority Status and Schooling: A Comparative Study of Immigrant and Involuntary Minorities*, New York: Garland Publishing, pp. 287–308.

Ladson-Billings G. (1990) 'Culturally relevant teaching: Effective instruction for Black students', *College Board Review* , **155**, pp. 20–25.

References

Ladson-Billings, G. (1994) *The Dreamkeepers: Successful Teachers of African American Children*, San Francisco, CA: Jossey-Bass.

Ladson-Billings, G. and Henry, A. (1990) 'Blurring the borders: Voices of African liberatory pedagogy in the United States and Canada', *Journal of Education*, **172**, 2, pp. 72–88.

Lawrence-Lightfoot, S. (1983) *A Good High School*, New York: Basic Books.

Lawrence-Lightfoot, S. (1994) *I've Known Rivers: Lives of Loss and Liberation*, Boston, MA: Addison-Wesley.

Lee, C. D. and Slaughter-Defoe, D. T. (1995) 'Historical and Sociocultural Influences on African American Education', in Banks, J. A. and Banks, C. A. M., (Eds.), *Handbook on Research on Multicultural Education*, New York: Macmillan, pp. 348–371.

Lee, J. F. J. (1991) *Asian Americans*, New York: New Press.

Lee, S. J. (1994) 'Behind the model-minority stereotype: Voices of high- and low-achieving Asian American students', *Anthropology and Education Quarterly*, **25**, 4, pp. 413–429.

Lee, Y. (1991) 'Koreans in Japan and the United States', in Gibson, M. A. and Ogbu, J. U. U., (Eds.), *Minority Status and Schooling: A Comparative Study of Immigrant and Involuntary Minorities*, New York: Garland Publishing, pp. 131–167.

Little, W. J. (1989) 'Conditions and forces influencing educational reform', in Braun, J. A., (Ed.), *Reforming Teacher Education*, New York: Garland.

Lomawaima, K. T. (1993) 'Domesticity in the federal Indian schools: The power of authority over mind and body', *American Ethnologist*, **20**, 2, pp. 1–14.

Lomawaima, K. T. (1995) 'Educating Native Americans', in Banks, J. A. and Banks, C. A. M., (Eds.), *Handbook on Research on Multicultural Education*, New York: Macmillan, pp. 331–347.

Lortie, D. C. (1975) *Schoolteacher: A Sociological Study*, Chicago, IL: University of Chicago Press.

McCullough-Garrett, A. (1993) 'Reclaiming the African American vision for teaching: Toward an educational conversation', *Journal of Negro Education*, **62**, 4, pp. 433–440.

Marashio, P. (1982) 'Enlighten my mind …. examining the learning process through Native Americans' ways', *Journal of American Indian Education*, **21**, 2, pp. 2–10.

Matute-Bianchi, M. E. (1991) 'Situational ethnicity and patterns of school performance among immigrant and nonimmigrant Mexican-descent students', in Gibson, M. A. and Ogbu, J. U. U., (Eds.), *Minority Status and Schooling: A Comparative Study of Immigrant and Involuntary Minorities*, New York: Garland Publishing, pp. 205–247.

Metz, M. H. (1990) 'How social class differences shape teachers' work', in McLaughlin, M. W., Talbert, J. E., and Bascia, N., (Eds.), *The Contexts of Teaching in Secondary School: Teachers' Realities*, New York: Teachers College Press, pp. 40–110.

Mishler, E. G. (1986) *Research Interviewing: Context and Narrative*, Cambridge, MA: Harvard University Press.

Montero-Sieburth, M. (1989) 'Restructuring teachers' knowledge for urban settings', *Journal of Negro Education*, **58**, 3, pp. 332–344.

Moore, J. W. and Pachon, H. (1985) *Hispanics in the United States*, Englewood Cliffs, NJ: Prentice-Hall.

Morris, V. G., Morris, C. L., and Taylor, S. I. (1998) 'We Did It Once, Can We Do It Again? Creating Caring and Nurturing Educational Environments for African American Children', Paper presented at American Educational Research Association, San Diego, CA.

Murnane, R. J., Singer, J. D., Willett, J. B., Kemple, J. J., and Olsen, R. J. (1991) *Who Will Teach? Policies That Matter*, Cambridge, MA: Harvard University Press.

Nabokov, P. (1991) *Native American Testimony: A Chronicle of Indian–White Relations From Prophecy to the Present, 1492–1992*, New York: Penguin Books.

Nakanishi, D. T. and Nishida, T. Y. (1995) *The Asian American Educational Experience: A Source Book for Teachers and Students*, New York: Routledge.

Ogbu, J. U. U. (1974) *The Next Generation: An Ethnography of Education in an Urban Neighborhood*, New York: Academic Press.

Ogbu, J. U. U. (1988) 'Cultural boundaries and minority youth orientation toward work preparation', in Stern, D. and Eichorn, D., (Eds.), *Adolescents and Work: Influences of Social Structure, Labor Markets and Culture*, Hillsdale, NJ: Lawrence Erlbaum Associates

Ogbu, J. U. U. (1990) 'Minority education in comparative perspective', *Journal of Negro Education*, **59**, 1, pp. 45–56.

Ogbu, J. U. U. (1991) 'Immigrant and involuntary minorities in comparative perspective', in Gibson, M. A. and Ogbu, J. U. U., (Eds.), *Minority Status and Schooling: A Comparative Study of Immigrant and Involuntary Minorities*, New York: Garland Publishing, pp. 3–33.

Ogbu, J. U. U. (1995) 'Cultural problems in minority education: Their interpretations and consequences – Part one: Theoretical background', *The Urban Review*, **27**, 3, pp. 189–205.

Ogbu, J. U. U. and Simons, H. D. (1998) 'Voluntary and involuntary minorities: a cultural-ecological theory of school performance with some implications for education', *Anthropology and Education Quarterly*, **29**, 2, pp. 155–188.

Olneck, M. R. and Lazerson, M. (1988) 'The school achievement of immigrant children: 1900–1930', in McClellan, B. and Reese, W. J., (Eds.), *The Social History of Education*, Urbana, IL: University of Illinois Press, pp. 257–286.

Omi, M. and Winant, H. (1986) *Racial Formation in the United States From the 1960s to the 1980s*, New York: Routledge and Kegan Paul.

Orfield, G. (1994) 'The growth of segregation in American schools: Changing patterns of segregation and poverty since 1968', *Equity and Excellence in Education*, **27**, 1, pp. 5–8.

Orfield, G. and Eaton, S. E. (1996) *Dismantling Segregation: The Quiet Reversal of Brown Vs. Board of Education*, New York: New Press.

Perkins, L. M. (1989) 'The history of blacks in teaching: Growth and decline within the profession', in Warren, D., (Ed.), *American Teachers: Histories of a Profession at Work*, New York: Macmillan, pp. 344–369.

Peshkin, A. (1992) 'Whom shall the schools serve? Some dilemmas of local control in a rural school district', in Stevens, E. and Wood, G., (Eds.), *Justice, Ideology, and Education*, Second Edition, New York: McGraw-Hill, pp. 221–240.

Pettigrew, T. F. (1974) 'Racially separate or together?', in Epps, E. G., (Ed.), *Cultural Pluralism*, Chicago, IL: McCutchan, pp. 1–36.

Philipsen, M. (1994) 'The second promise of Brown', *The Urban Review*, **26**, 4, pp. 257–272.

References

Recruiting New Teachers, Inc. (1993) *Careers in Teaching Handbook*, Belmont, MA: Recruiting New Teachers.

Reyhner, J. A. (1982) 'The self-determined curriculum: Indian teachers as cultural translators', *Journal of American Indian Education*, **21**, 1, pp. 19–23.

Reyhner, J. A. (1991) 'The challenge of teaching minority students: An American Indian example', *Teaching Education*, **4**, 1, pp. 103–111.

Reyhner, J. A. (1992) 'American Indians out of school: A review of school-based causes and solutions', *Journal of American Indian Education*, **31**, 3, pp. 37–55.

Rist, R. C. (1970) 'Student social class and teacher expectations: The self-fulfilling prophecy in ghetto education', *Harvard Educational Review*, **40**, 3, pp. 416–451.

Robinson, P. (1981) *Perspectives on the Sociology of Education: An Introduction*, London: Routledge & Kegan Paul.

Rohlen, T. P. (1983) *Japan's High Schools*, Berkeley, CA: University of California Press.

Rong, X. L. and Preissle, J. (1997) 'The continuing decline in Asian American teachers', *American Educational Research Journal*, **34**, 2, pp. 267–293.

Rosaldo, R. (1989) *Culture and Truth: The Remaking of Social Analysis*, Boston, MA: Beacon Press.

Rumbaut, R. G. (1995) 'The new Californians: Comparative research findings on the educational progress of immigrant children', Chapter 2 in Rumbaut, R. G. and Cornelius, W. A., (Eds.), *California's Immigrant Children*, San Diego, CA: University of California Press.

Rury, J. L. (1989) 'Who became teachers? The social characteristics of teachers in American history', in Warren, D., (Ed.), *American Teachers: Histories of a Profession at Work*, New York: Macmillan, pp. 9–48.

Salinas, G. (1971) 'Mexican Americans and the desegregation of schools in the Southwest', *Houston Law Review*, **8**, 929, p. 948.

San Miguel, G. Jr and Valencia, R. R. (1998) 'From the Treaty of Guadalupe Hidalgo to Hopwood: The Educational Plight and Struggle of Mexican Americans in the Southwest', *Harvard Educational Review*, **68**, 3, pp. 353–412.

Sarason, S. B. (1993a) *The Case for Change: Rethinking the Preparation of Educators*, San Francisco, CA: Jossey Bass.

Sarason, S. B. (1993b) *You Are Thinking of Teaching?*, San Francisco, CA: Jossey Bass.

Schlechty, P. C., Ingwerson, D. W., and Brooks, T. I. (1989) 'Inventing professional development schools', *Educational Leadership*, November, pp. 28–32.

Schwartz, H. (1996) 'The Changing Nature of Teacher Education', in Sikula, J., (Ed.), *Handbook of Research in Teacher Education*, Second Edition, New York: Macmillan, pp. 3–13.

Shor, I. (1980) 'The working class goes to college', in Shor, I., (Ed.), *Critical Teaching in Everyday Life*, Boston, MA: South End Press, pp. 1–44.

Shorris, E. (1992) *Latinos: A Biography of the People*, New York: Norton.

Siddle-Walker, E. V. (1993) 'Interpersonal caring in the "good" segregated schooling of African-American children: Evidence from the case of Caswell County Training School', *The Urban Review*, **25**, 1, pp. 63–77.

Sikula, J. (1996) (Ed.), *Handbook of Research in Teacher Education*, Second Edition, New York: Macmillan.

Sizemore, B. A. (1986) 'The limits of the Black superintendency: A review of the literature', *Journal of Educational Equity and Leadership*, **6**, 3, pp. 180–208.

Sklar, H. (1995) *Chaos or Community*, Boston, MA: South End Press.

Smedley, A. (1999) *Race in North America: Origin and Evolution of a Worldview*, Boulder, CO: Westview.

Smith, D. E. (1994) 'Understanding individuals and families: A cross-cultural perspective', *Journal of Home Economics*, **86**, 1, pp. 3–8.

Solomon, P. R. (1992) *Black Resistance in High School: Forging a Separatist Culture*, Albany, NY: State University of New York Press.

Sowell, T. (1983) *The Economics and Politics of Race*, New York: William Morrow.

Spindler, G. D. (1987) *Education and the Cultural Process: Anthropological Approaches*, Prospect, IL: Waveland Press.

Spindler, G. D., Spindler, L., Williams, M., and Trueba, H. T. (1990) *The American Cultural Dialogue and Its Transmission*, Bristol, PA: Falmer Press.

Spring, J. H. (1994) *Deculturalization and the Struggle for Equality*, New York: McGraw-Hill.

Stack, C. B. (1974) *All Our Kin: Strategies for Survival in a Black Community*, New York: Harper & Row.

Stanfield, J. H. I. (1994) 'Ethnic Modeling in Qualitative Research', in Denzin, N. R. and Lincoln, Y. S., (Eds.), *Handbook of Qualitative Research*, Thousand Oaks, CA: Sage Publications, pp. 175–188.

Steele, C. M. (1992) 'Race and the schooling of Black Americans', *Atlantic Monthly*, **269**, 4, pp. 68–78.

Steinberg, S. (1996) *Beyond the Classroom: Why School Reform Has Failed and What Parents Need to Do*, New York: Simon and Schuster.

Stewart, J. Jr, Meier, K. J., and England, R. E. (1989) 'In quest of role models: Change in Black teacher representation in urban school districts, 1968–1986', *Journal of Negro Education*, **58**, 2, pp. 140–152.

Stiegelbauer, S. (1992) 'The individual is the community: The community is the world: Native elders talk about what young people need to know', Paper presented at the American Educational Research Association, San Francisco, CA.

Strober, M. H. and Tyack, D. B. (1980) 'Why do women teach and men manage? A report of research on schools', *Signs: Journal of Women In Culture and Society*, **5**, 3, pp. 494–503.

Su, Z., Goldstein, S., Suzuki, G., and Kim, T. (1997) 'Socialization of Asian Americans in human service professional schools: A comparative study', *Urban Education*, **32**, 2, pp. 279–303.

Suarez-Orozco, M. M. (1989) *Central American Refugees and U. S. High Schools: A Psychosocial Study of Motivation and Achievement*, Stanford, CA: Stanford University Press.

Suarez-Orozco, M. M. (1991) 'Immigrant adaptation to schooling: A Hispanic case', in Gibson, M. A. and Ogbu, J. U. U., (Eds.), *Minority Status and Schooling: A Comparative Study of Immigrant and Involuntary Minorities*, New York: Garland Publishing, pp. 37–61.

Suarez-Orozco, M. M. (1998) (Ed.), *Crossings: Mexican Immigration in Interdisciplinary Perspectives*, Cambridge, MA: Harvard University Press.

References

Swisher, K. and Hoisch, M. (1992) 'Dropping out among American Indians and Alaska Natives: A review of studies', *Journal of American Indian Education*, **31**, 2, pp. 3–23.

Takaki, R. (1989) *Strangers From a Different Shore: A History of Asian/Americans*, Boston, MA: Little, Brown and Co.

Tierney, W. G. (1992) *Minorities in Academe: The Native American Experience*, Norwood, NJ: Ablex.

Trueba, E. H. T. (1998) 'Critical ethnography and a Vygotskian pedagogy of hope: the empowerment of Mexican immigrant children', Paper presented at American Educational Research Association, San Diego, CA.

Trueba, H. T. (1989) *Raising Silent Voices: Educating the Linguistic Minorities for the 21st Century*, New York: Newbury House.

Trueba, H. T., Cheng, L., and Ima, K. (1993) *Myth or Reality: Adaptive Strategies of Asian Americans in California*, Washington, DC: Falmer Press.

Tyack, D. B. (1987) 'An American tradition: The changing role of schooling and teaching', *Harvard Educational Review*, **57**, 2, pp. 171–174.

Unger, S. (1977) *The Destruction of American Indian Families*, New York: Association of American Indian Affairs.

Valdes, G. (1998) 'The World Outside and Inside Schools: Language and Immigrant Children', *Educational Researcher*, **27**, 6, pp. 4–18.

Valverde, S. A. (1987) 'A comparative study of Hispanic high school dropouts and graduates: Why do some leave school early and some finish?', *Education in Urban Society*, **19**, 3, pp. 320–329.

Vegas, E., Murnane, R. J., and Willett, J. B. (1998) 'From High School to Teaching: Many Steps. Who Makes It?', Paper presented at American Educational Research Association, San Diego, CA.

Wahab, Zaher (1989) '"The melting pot" revisited', Annual Conference of the Oregon Multicultural Association, Salem, Oregon.

Waller, W. (1932) *The Sociology of Teaching*, New York: John Wiley & Sons.

Warren, D. (1989) (Ed.), *American Teachers: Histories of a Profession at Work*, New York: Macmillan.

Weiler, K. (1988) *Women Teaching for Change*, South Hadley, MA: Bergin & Garvey.

Wilds, D. J. and Wilson, R. (1998) *Minorities in Higher Education*, Washington, DC: American Council on Education.

Willie, C. V. (1978) *The Sociology of Urban Education*, Boston, MA: Lexington Books.

Willis, P. (1977) *Learning to Labour: How Working Class Kids Get Working Class Jobs*, Aldershot: Gower Press.

Wilson, A. (1996) 'How we find ourselves: Identity development and two-spirit people', *Harvard Educational Review*, **66**, 2, pp. 303–317.

Wilson, W. J. (1991) 'Studying inner-city social dislocations: The challenge of public agenda research', *American Sociological Review*, **56**, pp. 1–14.

Yao, E. L. (1988) 'Working effectively with Asian immigrant parents', *Phi Delta Kappan*, **70**, 3, pp. 223–225.

Yee, S. M. (1990) *Careers in the Classroom: When Teaching is More Than a Job*, New York: Teachers College Press.

Zeichner, K. M. and Hoeft, K. (1996) 'Teacher Socialization for Cultural Diversity', in Sikula, J., (Ed.), *Handbook of Research in Teacher Education*, Second Edition, New York: Macmillan, pp. 525–547.

Zerfoss, Evelyn and Shapiro, Leo J. (1974) 'The supply and demand of teachers and teaching', Omaha, NE: University of Nebraska Printing Office.

Index